New American STREAMLINE

BERNARD HARTLEY & PETER VINEY

DEPARTURES

Ninia Viyua

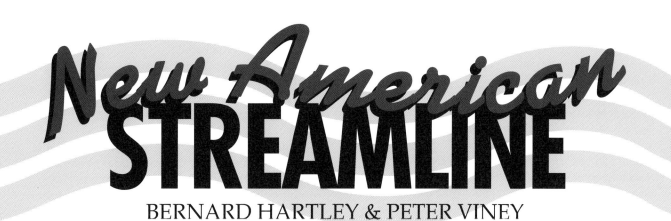

New American STREAMLINE

BERNARD HARTLEY & PETER VINEY

DEPARTURES

An intensive American English series for beginners
Student Book

REVISED BY PETER VINEY

Oxford University Press

Oxford University Press

198 Madison Avenue
New York, NY 10016 USA

Great Clarendon Street
Oxford OX2 6DP England

Oxford New York
Athens Auckland Bangkok Bogotá Buenos Aires
Calcutta Cape Town Chennai Dar es Salaam
Delhi Florence Hong Kong Istanbul Karachi
Kuala Lumpur Madrid Melbourne Mexico City
Mumbai Nairobi Paris São Paulo Singapore
Taipei Tokyo Toronto Warsaw

and associated companies in
Berlin Ibadan

OXFORD is a trademark of Oxford University Press

Library of Congress Cataloging-in-Publication Data

Hartley, Bernard.
New American streamline—departures: an intensive American English course for beginners: student
book / Bernard Hartley and Peter Viney.
p. cm.
"Based on the American adaptation by Flamm/
Northam Authors and Publishers Services, Inc."
ISBN 0-19-434825-3 (student bk.). — ISBN 0-19-
434827-X (teacher's bk.). — ISBN 0-19-434828-8 (cassette). — ISBN 0-19-434847-4 (CD)
1. English language—Textbooks for foreign speakers. 2. English language—United States.
3. Americanisms. I. Viney, Peter.
PE1128.H375   1994
428.2'4—dc20   93-23028

Based on the American adaptation by Flamm/
Northam Authors and Publishers Services, Inc.

Printing (last digit) 10 9 8

Printed in Hong Kong.

Editorial Manager: Susan Lanzano
Editor: Ken Mencz
Designer: Sharon Hudak
Art Buyer: Tracy Hammond/Gregory Ilich/
    Alexandra F. Rockafellar
Picture Researcher: Paul Hahn
Production Manager: Abram Hall

Cover illustration by: Pete Kelly

Illustrations and realia by: Ray Alma, Chris Costello,
Dee Deloy, John Edens, Sharon Hudak, Valerie
Marsella, Anthony Martin, Peg McGovern, Paddy
Mounter, Rebecca Perry, Tom Powers, Tim Raglin,
Jeff Seaver, Jeff Shelly, Anne Stanley, Stephan Van
Litsenborg

*The publisher would like to thank the following for their per-
mission to reproduce photographs:* Kul Bhatia/Photo
Researchers, Ron Calamia/Greater New Orleans
Tourist and Convention Commission, Tom Campbell/
FPG International, Denver Metro Convention and
Visitors Bureau, FPG International, Frederica Georgia/
Photo Researchers, Ned Haines/Photo Researchers,
Jan Halaska/Photo Researchers, Masao Hayashi/
Dunq/Photo Researchers, Paolo Koch/Photo
Researchers, Gary Levielle, Larry Mulvehill/Photo
Researchers, Porterfield/Chickering/Photo
Researchers, H. Armstrong Roberts, Don Spiro/The
Stock Shop, Superstock, Alain Thomas/Explorer/
Photo Researchers, Arthur Tress/Photo Researchers,
Uniphoto, Ulrike Welsch/Photo Researchers, ©Mike
Yamashita

Photography by: Richard Haynes, Milton Heiberg,
Cynthia Hill, Stephen Ogilvy

(If notified, the publisher will be pleased to rectify any
errors or omissions at the earliest opportunity.)

The publisher would like to thank the following companies:
AeroMexico; Air-India; Alitalia; All Nippon Airways;
American Express; American Honda Motor Co.; The
Boeing Company; Chevrolet/General Motors
Corporation; Concorde; CN Tower; Diners Club
International Ltd.; EPCOT® Center; Disney-MGM
Studios Theme Park; Ford Motor Company; Korean
Air; Los Angeles Times; Maid of the Mists Plaza;
MAGIC KINGDOM® Park; MasterCard International;
MCA Universal Studio; Minolta Corporation; Minolta
Tower Centre; National Broadcasting Company, Inc.
(WNBC); The New York Times; The Niagara Parks
Commission; NYNEX; Pacific Bell; Panasonic; The
Rainbow Bridge; Red Cross; Rolls-Royce Motor Cars
Inc.; The Skylon Tower; Table Rock House; Time Inc.;
Timex Corporation; United Airlines; Varig; Visa USA;
WABC; Walt Disney Company; WCBS; WNET; Zenith
Electronics Corporation
(All brands and product names are registered trade-
marks of their respective companies.)

Students can buy a cassette or CD which
contains a recording of the texts and dialogues in this book.

Hello

Hola

Speech bubbles:
- Hello. *Hola*
- Hello. *Hola*
- Are you a teacher? *Ares Un Maestro*
- No, I'm not.
- I'm David Clark. *yo soy David cla*
- I'm Linda Rivera. *yo soy linda Rivera*
- Oh, are you a student? *ohr, eres un stu*
- Yes, I am.

A B C D

Exercise 1

David Clark
Linda Rivera

He's David Clark.
She's Linda Rivera.

Alan Lee
Susan Lee

He's Alan Lee
She's Linda Rivera

John Green
Carol Green

He's John Green
She's Carol Green

Exercise 2

Is she a teacher?
No, she isn't.
Is she a student?
Yes, she is.

Are you a student?
No, *I'm not.*
or are you a teacher?
Yes, *I am* .

Exercise 3

Is he from the   • • • France?
United States?   No, • • • •.
No, he isn't.   • • • •?
Where's he from?   • • • Mexico.
He's from Canada.

• • • Brazil?
• • • •.
• • • •?
• • • Japan.

Exercise 4

Are you a
  teacher?
• • • •.
Are you a
  student?
• • • •.
Are you from the
  United States?
• • • •.
Where are you
  from?
• • • •.

Excuse me!

compermiso

I: Excuse me!
J: Yes?
I: Are you American?
J: Pardon me?
I: Are you from the United States?
J: Yes, we are.
I: Oh. I'm American too. Are you here on vacation?
J: No, we aren't. We're here on business.

J: Please sit down.
I: Thank you.

J: Coffee?
I: Yes, please.

J: Cream?
I: No, thanks.
J: Sugar?
I: Yes, please.

K: Where are you from?
I: I'm from Los Angeles.
K: Are you here on business?
I: No, I'm not. I'm on vacation.

Where are you from?

De donde eres.

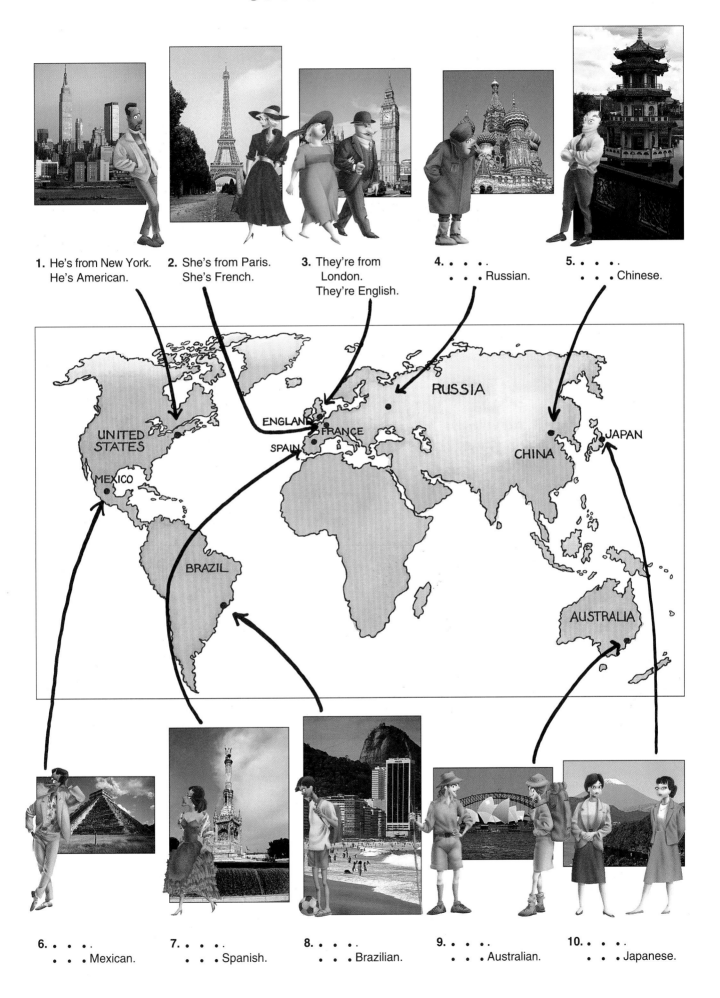

1. He's from New York. He's American.

2. She's from Paris. She's French.

3. They're from London. They're English.

4. . . . . Russian.

5. . . . . Chinese.

RUSSIA

ENGLAND
FRANCE
SPAIN

UNITED STATES

MEXICO

BRAZIL

CHINA

JAPAN

AUSTRALIA

6. . . . . Mexican.

7. . . . . Spanish.

8. . . . . . . Brazilian.

9. . . . . Australian.

10. . . . . Japanese.

What is it?

Que es esto

Anna: What is it? Is it a fly?
Mike: No, it isn't.
Anna: Is it a mosquito?
Mike: Uh…. Yes. Yes, it is.
Anna: Oh, no! It isn't a mosquito, Mike. It's a bee!

Exercise 1

Example:
a car . R .
an egg . M .

a glass . E .
a table . X .
a bus . S .
an apple . N .
a purse . J .
a knife . B .
a key . G .
a chair . W .
a train . U .
an iron . L .
a plate . C .
a cup . F .
an umbrella . K .
a window . Y .
a watch . H .
a spoon . A .
an orange . O .
a fork . D .
a shelf . Z .
a truck . T .
a pen . I .
a door . V .
a lemon . P .
a taxi . Q .

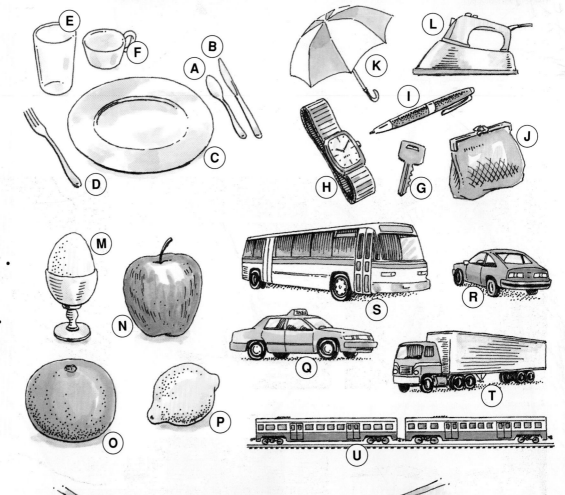

What are they?

Que son ellas

Exercise 2

1. They're forks.
2. They're cups.
3. They're cars.
4. They're keys.
5. They're glasses.
6. They're watches.
7. They're trucks.
8. They're knives.

Use these words:
watches
cups
knives
keys
trucks
cars
glasses

Exercise 3

1. What is it?
   It's a clock.

2. What are they?
   They're radios.

3. What is it?
   It's a airplane.

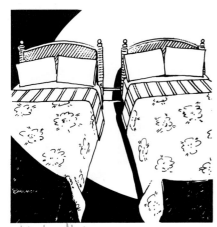

4. What are they
   They're beds.

5. What are they?
   They're houses.

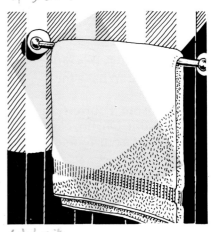

6. What is it?
   It's a towel.

What's your name?

Cual es tu nombre

Mr. Stern: Good evening.
Desk clerk: Good evening, sir. What's your name?
Mr. Stern: Stern. My name's Thomas Stern.
Desk clerk: Oh, yes, Mr. Stern. Room 15. Here's your key.
Mr. Stern: Thank you.
Desk clerk: You're welcome.

Bell captain: Is this your suitcase?
Mr. Stern: No, it isn't.
Bell captain: Oh, is that your suitcase over there?
Mr. Stern: Yes, it is.

Mrs. Johnson: Good evening.
Desk clerk: Good evening. What are your names, please?
Mrs. Johnson: Johnson. Mr. and Mrs. Johnson.
Desk clerk: Oh, yes. Here's your key.

Bell captain: Are these your suitcases here?
Mr. Johnson: No, they aren't.
Bell captain: Oh, I'm sorry. Are those your suitcases over there?
Mr. Johnson: Yes, they are.

Mrs. Johnson: Is this our room?
Mr. Johnson: What's the number?
Mrs. Johnson: Fourteen.
Mr. Johnson: Oh, no. No, it isn't. That's our room—number 13!

What's your job?

Cual es tu trabajo (handwritten)

Exercise 1

Look at 13.
What's her job?
She's a hotel manager.

Look at 14.
What's his job?
He's a cashier.

Look at 15.
What are their jobs?
They're waiters.

Look at 16.
• • •?
• • • .

Look at 17.
• • •?
• • • .

Look at 18.
• • •?
• • • .

Look at 19.
• • •?
• • • .

Use these words:
secretary
cooks
housekeeper
bell captain

Homework. (handwritten)

Exercise 2

Look at 20.
What's his job?
He's a pilot.

21. • • •?
    • • • .
22. • • •?
    • • • .
23. • • •?
    • • • .
24. • • •?
    • • • .

Use these words:
police officers
flight attendants
taxi driver
mechanic

Exercise 3

What's your name?
• • • .

What's your job?
• • • .

I'm cold

Tengo Frio

A: Brr!
B: Are you cold?
A: Yes, I am.
B: Well, I'm not. I'm hot!

Exercise

Look at C.
Q: Is it big?
A: No, it isn't.
Q: Is it small?
A: Yes, it is.

Use these words:

Vino vacio
full/empty
bonito y feo beautiful/ugly
grueso y delgado thick/thin
barato y caro cheap/expensive

strong/weak *fuerte y devil*
long/short *largo y corto*
old/new *viejo y nuevo*
tall/short *alto y bajo*
old/young *viejo y joven*

Esta tarde

Listen to the conversations.
Put A, B, C... on the picture
on the right.

A: The plane's late. *Tarde*
B: Yes, it's very late.

C: Are they tired? *cansado*
D: No, they aren't tired. He's
hungry and she's thirsty. *hambre / sed*

E: They're tired.
F: Yes, they are.

G: This is terrible! I'm very
angry! *enfadado*
H: I'm sorry, ma'am.

I: Is that book good?
J: Yes, it is. But it's very sad. *Triste*

K: Phew! I'm hot!
L: Yes. That coat's very warm! *chaqueta*

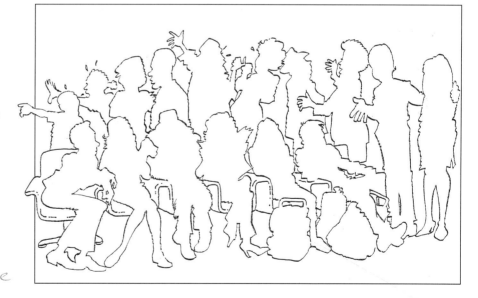

Exercise

1. It's *late.*   **2.** He's   **3.** She's   **4.** They're   **5.** She's   **6.** She's   **7.** He's   **8.** It's

hungry   thirsty *sed*   Tired *cansados*   angry *enfadada*   Sorry *Disculpa*   hot *caliente*   Sad- *Triste*

There's a nice apartment

Esto es un apartamento bonito.

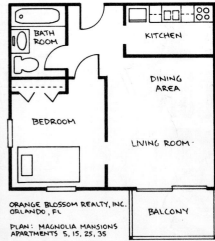

Realtor: This is a nice apartment, Ms. Garcia. Look, here's a floor plan.

Eva: Mmm….

Realtor: There's a living room. There's a kitchen, a bedroom, and a bathroom.

Eva: Is there a balcony?

Realtor: Yes, there is.

Eva: And a dining room…is there a dining room?

Realtor: No, there isn't a dining room. But there is a dining area in the living room.

Realtor: Well, this is the kitchen.

Eva: Oh, it's very small.

Realtor: Yes, it isn't very large. But there's a stove, a refrigerator, and a space for a dishwasher. There are some cabinets, and…um…there's a small shelf under the sink.

Eva: Are there any windows in the bathroom?

Realtor: No, there aren't. But there are two large windows in the bedroom.

Eva: Good. It's a very nice apartment. Uh, where *is* the bathroom?

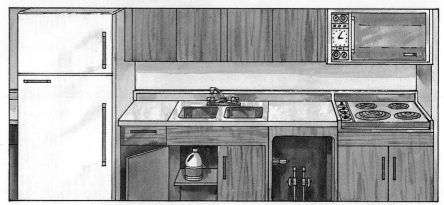

Homework

Exercise 1

sofa
There's a sofa in the living room.
VCR
There isn't a VCR in the living room.

Write sentences with:
1. telephone *teléfon*
2. chair *silla*
3. rug *Tapete.*
4. coffee table

Exercise 2

books
There are some books on the shelf.
cups
There aren't any cups on the shelf.

Write sentences with:
1. glasses *cristales*
2. compact discs *discos compactos*
3. magazines *revistas*
4. videocassettes *caset*

Exercise 3

telephone/coffee table?
Is there a telephone on the coffee table?
books/shelf
Are there any books on the shelf?

Write questions with:
1. radio/shelf
2. bottles/coffee table
3. compact discs/coffee table

Exercise 4

Where are the compact discs?
They're on the coffee table.
Where's the rug?
It's in the living room.

Answer the questions:
1. Where's the television?
2. Where are the glasses?
3. Where are the books?
4. Where's the sofa?

Requerir

A: Hi. A cola, please.
B: Regular or large?
A: Regular, please.
B: There you go.
A: Thanks. How much is that?
B: $1.15.
A: Thank you.
B: You're welcome.

	REG.	LARGE
COLA	$1.15	$1.50
DIET COLA		
ORANGE SODA		
LEMON/LIME SODA		
LEMONADE	$1.50	$2.50
COFFEE, TEA		$1.15

podrías pasarme

C: Could you pass the salt, please? *aquí esta*
A: Sure. Here you are.
C: Thanks.
A: And the pepper?
C: No, thanks.

C: Could I have your phone number?
A: It's in the phone book.
C: What's your last name?
A: It's in the book, too.
C: Very funny. *gracioso / Que gracioso*
A: OK. It's 639-7701.

836-6809
356 - 8022
296 - 2837
549 - 6244
688 - 2119
679 - 7300
639-7701

Make conversations:

Student 1:

Could you	pass	
Could I	have	(the bread)?

puedes tu pasar
puedes yo tener

Student 1:

Thank you.
Thanks.

Student 2:

There	you	go.
Here		are.

Student 2:

You're welcome.
That's OK.

bread

cream

milk

salad dressing   straws   sweetener

Uniformes

Listen. Find the people in the picture.

How do you do? My name's Tiffany Gonzales, and I'm a flight attendant for Air USA. This is my uniform—a blue skirt, a pink blouse, and a black jacket. It's very stylish.

Carlos da Silva is a soccer player for Brazil. His shirt is yellow and green, and his shorts are blue and white.

Hi there. I'm Brian…and I'm Diane. We're lifeguards at Bay Beach. Our uniforms aren't very stylish—white shorts, orange T-shirts, and green caps.

Adriana Papadopolos is a fire fighter in a small town in Kansas. Her jacket is red, her hat is brown, her pants are gray, and her boots are yellow.

Brandon Timmons and Jason Davis are baseball players for the Bayport Seagulls. Their pants are white, and their shirts are black and orange.

Exercise 1

Who's this?
It's Carlos da Silva.
He's a soccer player.

Who are they?
They're lifeguards. Their names are Brian and Diane.

Exercise 2

What color is her blouse?
It's pink.

What color are his pants?
They're white.

Exercise 3

Ask and answer about students in your class:
What color's his shirt?
What color's her dress?
What color are their shoes?

Exercise 4

Describe these people.
Use these words:
cape/tights/dress/apron/boots/mask

Whose is it?

De Quien es esto?

Dan: Hi there, Erica.
Erica: Hello, Dan. Wow! What's that?
Dan: It's a 1936 Cord.
Erica: It's beautiful! Is it your car?
Dan: No…no, it isn't.
Erica: Whose car is it?
Dan: It's Jessica Montana's car.
Erica: Jessica Montana? Who's she?
Dan: She's my boss.

Exercise 1

Who is it? It's Erica.

Write sentences for B and C.

Exercise 2

1. *What is it? It's a backpack.*
2. *What are they?*
   They're sunglasses. gafas o Antiojos

Write sentences for 3–12.

Exercise 3

1. *Whose backpack is it?*
   It's Erica's backpack.
2. *Whose sunglasses are they?*
   They're Jessica's sunglasses.

Write sentences for 3–12.

Look at this:

Look at Dick.
He's Anne's husband.
He's John's father.

Look at Anne.
She's Dick's wife.
She's Sue's mother.

Look at John.
He's their son.
He's Sue's brother.

Look at Sue.
She's their daughter.
She's John's sister.

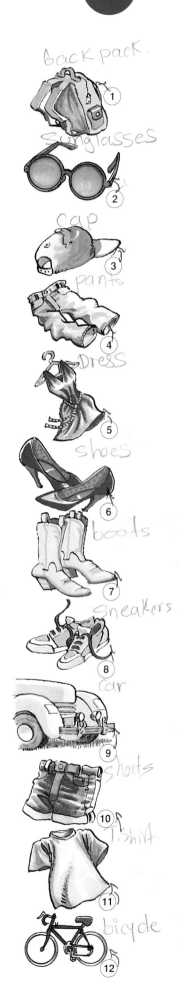

backpack. 1
sunglasses 2
cap 3
pants 4
Dress 5
shoes 6
boots 7
sneakers 8
car 9
shorts 10
T-shirt 11
bicycle 12

There's some oil in the bottle
Hay algo de aseite en la botella

Steve: Kelly! Where's the oil?
Kelly: What?
Steve: Where's the oil? There isn't any oil in the cabinet.
Kelly: There's some oil right there…in the bottle on the shelf.
Steve: OK. Sorry.

There's some oil in the bottle.

Write sentences with:

oil/bottle   sugar/bowl
water/pitcher   honey/jar
rice/box   milk/glass

Steve: Are there any onions?
Kelly: Sure.
Steve: Where are they?
Kelly: They're right here. There are some on the table.

There are some onions on the table.

Make conversations with:
apples/lemons/bananas/eggs/
oranges/tomatoes/mushrooms

There isn't anything in the refrigerator. It's empty!
There isn't any butter.
There aren't any tomatoes.

Write sentences with:
cheese/mushrooms/eggs/lemonade

Q: Is there any cheese in the refrigerator?
A: Yes, there is.

Q: Are there any eggs in the refrigerator?
A: Yes, there are.

Q: Is there any butter in the refrigerator?
A: No, there isn't.

Q: Are there any tomatoes in the refrigerator?
A: No, there aren't.

Write questions and answers with:
milk/salad dressing/
mushrooms/lemons

Exercise

bread
A: There's some bread in the freezer.
B: How much is there?
A: There's a lot.

Write conversations with:
ice cream
meat

hamburgers
A: There are some hamburgers in the freezer.
B: How many are there?
A: There are a lot.

Write conversations with:
peas
pizzas

Un Restaurant en America.

Customer: Waiter! I'd like the menu, please.
Waiter: There you go, sir.
Customer: Thanks…. I'd like some soup….
Waiter: Tomato soup?
Customer: Yes, and I'd like a steak.
Waiter: Rare, medium, or well-done?
Customer: Medium, please.
Waiter: Which vegetables would you like?
Customer: I'd like some potatoes, some peas…oh, and a green salad.
Waiter: Certainly, sir. Would you like dressing on your salad?
Customer: Please.
Waiter: Which salad dressing would you like, sir? French? Italian? Thousand Island? Oil and vinegar…?
Customer: Oil and vinegar, please.

Menu

APPETIZERS
ONION SOUP
TOMATO SOUP $2.90
FRIED MUSHROOMS $2.50
STUFFED TOMATOES $4.30
$2.60

ENTREES
SIRLOIN STEAK $14.80
ROAST BEEF $12.70
FRIED CHICKEN $10.90
FILET OF SOLE $11.50
HAM OMELETTE $9.30
CHEESE OMELETTE $8.60

VEGETABLES
ALL ENTREES COME WITH CHOICE OF:
BAKED POTATO OR MASHED POTATOES, PEAS, CARROTS, GREEN BEANS, OR BROCCOLI

SIDE DISHES
FRENCH FRIES $1.80
MIXED GREEN SALAD $2.40
SPINACH SALAD $2.20
CHOICE OF SALAD DRESSINGS: FRENCH, ITALIAN, THOUSAND ISLAND, OIL AND VINEGAR

DESSERTS
ICE CREAM $2.30
CHOICE OF CHOCOLATE, STRAWBERRY, OR VANILLA
APPLE PIE $2.10
CHOCOLATE CAKE $3.50

BEVERAGES
COFFEE $1.60
TEA $1.40
COLA $1.70

Exercise 1

A: How much is the steak?
B: It's fourteen dollars and eighty cents. 14·80
A: How much are the mushrooms?
B: They're four dollars and thirty cents. 4.30

Ask and answer about the menu.

Exercise 2

A: Which soup would you like?
B: I'd like the onion soup.

Ask and answer about the menu.

Computer game

Juego en computadora

03-28-01

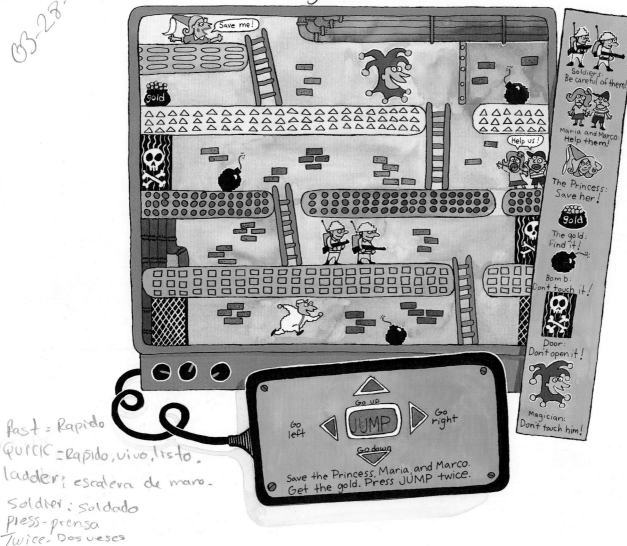

fast = Rapido
QUICK = Rapido, vivo, listo.
ladder: escalera de mano.
Soldier: Soldado
Press - prensa
Twice - Dos veses

Look at the instructions. Listen.

OK. That's you on the first level. Go right. Be careful. Don't touch the bomb! Stop. Jump! That's right. Now go up the ladder. Go right. Quick! Don't open the door. Go left. Jump! Be very careful. Jump again—don't touch the soldiers. Go up the ladder. Don't go left, go right. Jump! Don't go up the ladder. Jump again. Get Maria and Marco. Press "jump" twice. OK, now go back. Jump! Go up the ladder. Go right. Go left. Jump fast! Go up the ladder and save the princess. Press "jump" twice. Now, go down the ladder and go left. That's the gold. Press "jump" twice. OK, that's level one.

Exercise 1

Don't look at the instructions. Look at the picture above. Work with a partner. Give her/him instructions.

Robbie the Robot

Good. Listen to me, Robbie. Turn the vacuum cleaner off. That's right. Now, turn the TV on…. That's great! Now turn the TV off. Go to the door. Open it. Fantastic! Come here. Give me the newspaper. Thank you…. Go to the windows. Close them. Now go to the door. Go out. Walk to the front door. Open it. Go out and…Robbie! Robbie! Come back here! Robbie! Where are you? Robbie…!

Exercise 2

Work with a partner. Your partner is a robot. Give her/him instructions.

March 29 Quick

Quien esta feliz?

03-29-01

Look at this woman. Her name's Donna Walton. These are her three children, Jane, Darryl, and Michelle. Donna's an English teacher. She's not rich, and she's not famous.

Look at her house. It's small and there's no pool. There are three bedrooms in the house.

Donna's car is old. It's slow and uncomfortable. There's no radio or cassette player in her car. There's an engine, a steering wheel, and there are four wheels and two doors. Donna isn't happy. She'd like a big house, a new car, and a lot of money.

Look at this man. His name's Zach Zebedee. He's a rock star. He's very rich and famous. Look at his house. It's large and expensive, and there's a swimming pool in the backyard. There are ten bedrooms in the house.

Zach's car is new. It's a white Lincoln stretch limo. It's fast and comfortable. In his car there's a climate control system, a CD player, a VCR, a phone, and a fax machine.

But Zach isn't happy. He'd like a small house, a small car, and a family—with two kids.

Exercise

Zach's a rock star.   Donna's an English teacher.
Zach's famous.   • • •.
Zach's house is large.   • • •.
He'd like a family.   • • •.
Continue.

My dad can do everything!

Sally: My dad's really wonderful. He's big and strong and handsome.

Annie: Really? Well, *my* dad can do everything.

Sally: Can he? What?

Annie: He's really smart. He can speak a hundred languages.

Sally: A hundred! What languages can he speak?

Annie: Well, he can speak Spanish, Italian, French, German, Japanese, Arabic, and, uh, a lot more.

Sally: Well, my dad is very athletic.

Annie: Athletic?

Sally: Uh-huh. He can swim, ski, and play football, tennis, and baseball.

Annie: Oh, well, can your dad cook?

Sally: Cook? No, he can't.

Annie: My dad is a wonderful cook.

Sally: Really?

Annie: Yes, and he can paint and play the piano, too.

Sally: Oh. My dad can't do that. But my mom is beautiful and smart and she can….

Questions

1. Is Sally's father big?
2. Is he ugly?
3. Can he play football?
4. Can he play the piano?
5. Can he ski?
6. Can he cook?
7. Is Annie's father athletic?
8. Is he smart?
9. Can he speak Arabic?
10. Can he play tennis?
11. Can he paint?
12. Is Sally's mother smart?

Exercise

Example:
I can swim, but I can't ski.

Write ten sentences.

G: Please come in.
H: Thank you.
G: Sit down.
H: Thanks.
G: Would you like tea or coffee?
H: A cup of coffee, please.
G: How about a cookie?
H: No, thanks. I'm on a diet.

a cup of coffee
a cup of tea
a glass of water
a glass of milk
a can of soda
a bottle of mineral water

a cookie
a sandwich
a piece of cake
a piece of candy
a piece of fruit

I: Excuse me....
J: Yes, can I help you?
I: I'd like a pair of shoes, please.
J: What color would you like?
I: Brown.
J: What size are you?
I: Seven. Can I try them on?
J: Sure.

a pair of shoes
a pair of sneakers
a pair of jeans
a pair of boots

a sweater
a jacket
a raincoat

K: Hi. A frozen yogurt, please.
L: What flavor? Strawberry, chocolate, or vanilla?
K: Strawberry, please.
L: In a sugar cone or in a cup?
K: In a cup, please.
L: There you go. That's a dollar ninety-five.

a frozen yogurt
an ice-cream cone
a milk shake
an ice-cream float

in a cup/in a sugar cone
to stay (eat in)/ to go (take out)
in a paper cup/ in a glass

$1.95/$1.85/ $2.25/$2.35

Look at the picture and make conversations.

What do they have?

Que tienen ellos

Hi there, fans. My name's Courtney Dallas. I'm a famous actress—a superstar! I'm from Los Angeles. I have an apartment in New York and a house in Hollywood with a swimming pool and a tennis court. I have a new Mercedes© and a lot of money in the bank. I'm married and I have three wonderful children. I have everything. Life's great!

gran vida.

Hello. My name's Ike Proudfoot. I'm from Alaska. I have a small cabin in the woods. I don't have a car, a TV, a radio, or a phone. I don't have a job, I don't have any money, and I don't have a family. I don't have anything, but life's fantastic out here.

Hello there. Our names are Tina and Chuck Jackson. We're from Chicago. I'm a nurse and Chuck has a job in a factory. We don't have a big house, but we have a nice apartment. We have two cars. I have a new Honda. Chuck doesn't have a new car. He has an old Chevrolet. It's beautiful. And we have two great kids. Life's good.

Exercise 1

Example: house in Hollywood
Does she have a house in Hollywood?
Yes, she does.

1. swimming pool
2. tennis court
3. Mercedes
4. three children

Exercise 3

Example:
brother   *I have a brother.*
Mercedes   *I don't have a Mercedes.*

Write four sentences:
1. passport
2. watch
3. motorcycle
4. color TV

Exercise 2

Example: a job
Does he have a job? No, he doesn't.

1. a house
2. a car
3. a TV
4. any money
5. any children

Exercise 4

Answer these questions with *Yes, I do* or *No, I don't.*

1. Do you have a car?
2. Do you have a passport?
3. Do you have any children?
4. Do you have a watch?
5. Do you have any money?

Questions

1. What are their names?
2. Where are they from?
3. What are their jobs?
4. Does Chuck have a new car?
5. Does he have a Chevrolet or a Honda?
6. Do they have an apartment?
7. Do they have any children?

Exercise 5

Write questions. Ask a partner the questions.

1. computer?
2. calculator?
3. VCR?
4. any compact discs?
5. any videocassettes?

pagina para examen. *Slaves = esclavos.*

La. Aduana.

guilty = culpable.

Customs Officer: Good morning. May I see your passport?

Ralph: Sure. Here it is.

C.O.: Thank you. Hmm. OK. Do you have anything to declare?

Ralph: No, I don't.

C.O.: You have six suitcases. Is that right?

Ralph: Yes, that's right.

C.O.: What do you have in your cases?

Ralph: Clothes. And I have some compact discs and some perfume.

C.O.: How much perfume do you have?

Ralph: One bottle.

C.O.: OK. And how many CDs do you have?

Ralph: Um…three.

C.O.: Fine. Do you have anything else?

Ralph: No, I don't.

C.O.: Good. Now open this suitcase, please.

Ralph: Huh? What?

C.O.: Open your suitcase. Now, let's see. Well, look at this. You have three portable CD players, five…no, six large bottles of perfume, and a lot of CDs.

Questions

1. How many suitcases does Ralph have? *he has*
2. Does he have any CD players? *yes he has a lot cd player*
3. Ask, "How many?"
4. Does he have any perfume? *yes he has perfume*
5. Ask, "How much?"
6. Does he have any CDs? *yes he has a lot CD*
7. Ask, "How many?"

Exercise

How much perfume does she have?
How many cameras does she have?

Write four questions:
1. *How much* gold *she has? a lot gold*
2. *How much* money *she has? a lot money*
3. *How many* rings *Does she has a lot rings*
4. *How many* watches *Does she has? has 3 watches*

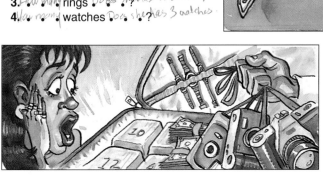

Which one?

Lucy: Hi, George. It's a great party.

George: Thank you. How about some more salad?

Lucy: Thanks.

George: Which plate is yours?

Lucy: That one's mine.

George: Which one?

Lucy: The empty one!

George: Charles and Lucy would like some more coffee.

Linda: OK. Which mugs are theirs?

George: Uh, the blue one's his, and the white one's hers.

Linda: Are you sure?

George: Um, I don't know.

Linda: George! Give them fresh mugs. There are some on the shelf.

Charles: Good night and thanks for a lovely evening.

George: Now, which coats are yours?

Charles: Those coats are ours.

George: Which ones?

Charles: The black one and the gray one.

George: Ah, yes....

Charles: Thanks. The gray one's mine, and the black one's hers.

Exercise 1

cookie
Which one would you like? I'd like the small one.
1. ice-cream cone   chocolate/vanilla
2. pizza   hot/cold
3. apple   red/green

Exercise 2

pens
Which ones would you like?
I'd like the blue ones.
1. envelopes   small/large
2. notepads   plain/lined
3. computers   black and white/ color

Exercise 3

Example:
It's my pen.   *It's mine.*
They're our books.   *They're ours.*

1. It's his car.
2. It's their house.
3. It's Michael's coat.
4. It's her hat.

5. It's your house.
6. It's Maria's bag.
7. They're our friends.
8. They're your pens.

(handwritten notes at top: página para examen / April 23 / Monday - Quiz / units 14-19 / May 4th - Friday - final / on everything #-25)

M: Excuse me.
N: May I help you?
M: I'd like some information about the trains.
N: Where to?
M: Montreal.
N: When?
M: Tomorrow.
N: Morning or afternoon?
M: Evening. Around six o'clock.
N: OK. There's one at 6:40.
M: Thanks.

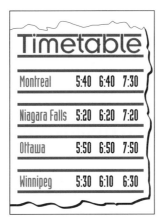

Timetable			
Montreal	5:40	6:40	7:30
Niagara Falls	5:20	6:20	7:20
Ottawa	5:50	6:50	7:50
Winnipeg	5:30	6:10	6:30

O: Excuse me, is this seat taken?
P: No, it isn't.
O: Is it OK if I sit here?
P: Yes, of course.
O: Is that your newspaper?
P: Yes, it is.
O: May I borrow it for a minute?
P: Yes, sure.

Q: Good morning. May I see your ticket, please?
R: Yes. Here it is.
Q: OK. Do you have any luggage?
R: Yes, one suitcase.
Q: Put it right here.
R: Can I carry it on the plane with me? It isn't heavy.
Q: No, I'm sorry. It's the wrong size.

GOOD MORNING.
GOOD AFTERNOON.
GOOD EVENING.

Look at the departures boards and practice conversations:

A: Excuse me.

B: Yes,	sir.	May	I help you?
	ma'am.	Can	

A: Which	track	is the	Oakland	train,	please?
	gate		Chicago	flight,	

B: The	9:30	is	on track	eighteen.
	3:50		at gate	sixteen.

A:	Sorry. Is that (eight) or (eighteen)?

B:	(Eighteen).

TRAIN DEPARTURES	TIME NOW 9:08	
DESTINATION	TIME	TRACK
ST. LOUIS	9:10	29
WASHINGTON	9:20	7
OAKLAND	9:30	18
MINNEAPOLIS	9:40	8
NEW YORK CITY	9:50	17

FLIGHT DEPARTURES		TIME NOW 3:17	
FLIGHT#	DESTINATION	GATE	TIME
FL349	Orlando	4	3:20
SC168	New Orleans	19	3:30
CE411	Vancouver	6	3:40
TG572	Chicago	16	3:50
SE902	Atlanta	14	4:00
TG705	Mexico City	9	4:10

St. Augustine, Florida

Denver, Colorado

Look at these facts. Which ones are about St. Augustine and which ones are about Denver?
<u>Underline</u> the facts about St. Augustine.

* It's on the Atlantic Ocean.
* It's near the Rocky Mountains.
* It's a modern city (first houses in 1858).
* It's an old town (built 1565, the first town in North America).
* There are a lot of old Spanish buildings.
* It's 1,600 meters above sea level.
* There are some beautiful old churches.
* There are some military bases in the city.
* It's very cold in winter.
* It has a population of half a million.

* It's a center for winter sports.
* You can find gold and silver in the area.
* It has a large airport.
* The weather is hot in the summer, warm in winter.
* There are two rivers in the city.
* There's an old Spanish fortress.
* Tourism is very important in this small town.
* There are two universities and a lot of colleges in the town.
* It has a population of around 12,000.
* It's the state capital of Colorado.

Ask another student questions:

Does Denver have a population of 12,000?
Can you find gold near St. Augustine?
Are there a lot of old Spanish buildings in Denver?

Ask your teacher the answers!

Which city would **you** like to visit?
Denver or St. Augustine? Why?

Exercise 1

Write eight sentences about your town.

Exercise 2

Write a postcard from **your** town.

Dear Wendy,

This is a picture of New Orleans. It's very hot here, and there's a lot of rain. It's a very beautiful city with lovely old buildings in the French Quarter. It's on the Mississippi River. The river is very wide! The food is excellent. There are a lot of seafood restaurants. You can hear jazz music everywhere. You'd like it here very much.

See you soon.

Best wishes,
Steven

Ms. Wendy Bonikoff

14160 S. Bluff

White Rock

British Columbia

V42 3E6

Canada

What are they doing?

Que estan haciendo ellos.

Laura: Hello.

Jamie: Hello, Laura. Is Scott there?

Laura: Oh, hi, Jamie. Yes, he is. But he's busy.

Jamie: Is he working?

Laura: No, he isn't working. He's in the kitchen.

Jamie: What's he doing?

Laura: He's cooking.

Jamie: What are you doing?

Laura: I'm reading.

Questions

1. Is Scott working?
2. What's he doing?
3. Is Laura cooking?
4. What's she doing?

Look at the picture.

Exercise 1

She's cooking.
She's drinking.
He's sleeping.
They're dancing.
She's singing.
They're eating.

Exercise 2

G. *What's he doing? He's writing.*

H. *What's she doing? She's reading.*

I. *What's he doing? He's writing.*

J. *What's she doing? She's typing.*

drawing/typing/reading

Look at these words:

work	working	dance	dancing
cook	cooking	write	writing
read	reading	type	typing
eat	eating		
drink	drinking		
sing	singing	sit	sitting
sleep	sleeping	run	running
draw	drawing	swim	swimming

Exercise 3

swimming/eating

He's swimming.
She isn't swimming.
Is she eating? *Yes, she is.*
Is he eating? *No, he isn't.*

reading/writing

Can you help me?

puedes ayudarme

Carlos is a student. He's staying with the Flynns, a family in Boston.

Carlos: Mrs. Flynn, can you help me? I'm doing my homework, and I can't understand this word.

Mrs. Flynn: Which one? Oh, that's difficult. I'm sorry, Carlos. I can't help you now. I'm watching TV. I can help you later.

Carlos: Oh? What are you watching?

Mrs. Flynn: I'm watching an old Western with Clint Eastwood.

Carlos: Can Mr. Flynn help me?

Mrs. Flynn: Well, no, he can't. Not now. He's reading.

Carlos: What's he reading?

Mrs. Flynn: He's reading a magazine.

Carlos: What about Kate?

Mrs. Flynn: Oh, she can't help you now. She's talking on the phone.

Carlos: Who's she talking to?

Mrs. Flynn: I don't know. You're asking a lot of questions tonight, Carlos!

Carlos: Yes, I know. I'm practicing my English.

Exercise

Jill and John/tennis.
What are Jill and John *doing?*
They're playing tennis.

Mr. and Mrs. Nelson/television
Kate/her car
Mr. Wilson/a letter
Kenji/a letter
Debbie and Joe/a box
Tony/coffee

watching   *mirando*
drinking   *Tomando*
carrying   *cargando*
washing   *lavando*
writing   *escribiendo*
typing   *mecanografiando*

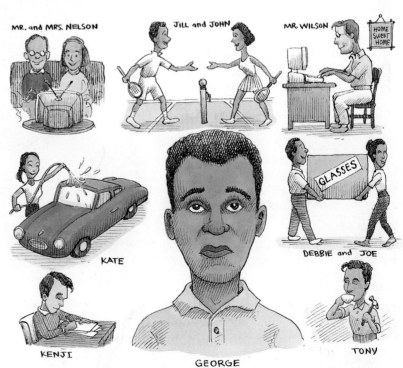

George is lonely and unhappy. His friends are busy today.

Shopping
Comprando

S: Can I help you?
T: Pardon me?
S: Can I help you?
T: Oh, no thanks. I'm just looking.

Can I...?
May I...?

Pardon me?
Excuse me?

U: Can you show me some cameras, please?
V: Sure. What make do you want?
U: I'd like a Minolta.
V: This one's very good. It's a new model.
U: How much is it?
V: $180.
U: Oh, that's too expensive.
V: How much can you spend?
U: Around $100.
V: Here's one at $99.50.
U: Great! Can you show it to me?

cameras (Minolta)
CD players (Panasonic)
watches (Timex)
color TVs (Zenith)

$180/$100/$99.50
$185/$160/$162
$53/$30/$28.75
$500/$400/$250

W: Good morning.
X: Good morning. How may I help you?
W: I'm looking for a textbook.
X: What's the title?
W: *Instant English.* Do you have it?
X: Yes. It's over here.
W: How much is it?
X: $12.00.
W: May I see it, please?
X: Sure. There you go.
W: Thank you.
X: Your English is very good. Are you studying it?
W: No. I'm teaching it!

book (*Instant English*)
CD (*Rap Hits*)
magazine (*Time*)
cassette (*English in 20 Minutes*)
dictionary (*New Oxford Picture Dictionary*)

$12.00
$15.99
$2.95
$13.99
$18.95

Exercise
Homework

Number the sentences below and make a conversation.

Student A	Student B
That's too much.	What make would you like?
Around $75.	How much do you want to spend?
Could you show it to me?	Hello. Can I help you? 2
Hello.	Sure.
I don't know.	$150.
OK. What's the price?	I have this one at $89.95.
I'm looking for a personal stereo.	This Sony's very good.

The fashion show

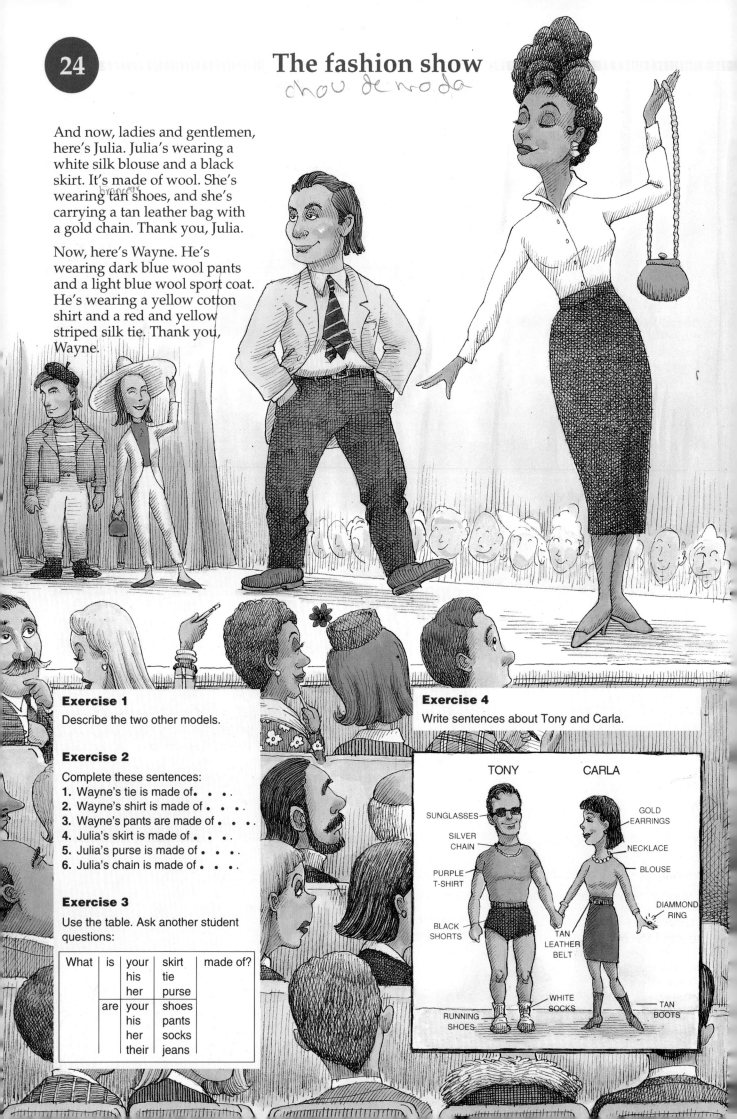

And now, ladies and gentlemen, here's Julia. Julia's wearing a white silk blouse and a black skirt. It's made of wool. She's wearing tan shoes, and she's carrying a tan leather bag with a gold chain. Thank you, Julia.

Now, here's Wayne. He's wearing dark blue wool pants and a light blue wool sport coat. He's wearing a yellow cotton shirt and a red and yellow striped silk tie. Thank you, Wayne.

Exercise 1

Describe the two other models.

Exercise 2

Complete these sentences:
1. Wayne's tie is made of. . . .
2. Wayne's shirt is made of . . . .
3. Wayne's pants are made of . . . .
4. Julia's skirt is made of . . . .
5. Julia's purse is made of . . . .
6. Julia's chain is made of . . . .

Exercise 3

Use the table. Ask another student questions:

What	is	your	skirt	made of?
		his	tie	
		her	purse	
	are	your	shoes	
		his	pants	
		her	socks	
		their	jeans	

Exercise 4

Write sentences about Tony and Carla.

TONY — SUNGLASSES, SILVER CHAIN, PURPLE T-SHIRT, BLACK SHORTS, RUNNING SHOES, WHITE SOCKS

CARLA — GOLD EARRINGS, NECKLACE, BLOUSE, DIAMOND RING, TAN LEATHER BELT, TAN BOOTS

Victor's standing outside the movie theater. He's waiting for his friend Tania. He's looking at his watch because she's late. An old man's coming out of the theater. A young woman's going into the theater. A boy's running up the steps. A woman's buying a ticket from the cashier. Some people are standing in line outside the movie theater.

Questions

Where's Victor standing?
Who's he waiting for?
What's he looking at?
Why is he looking at his watch?
Who's coming out of the theater?
Who's going into the theater?
Where's the boy running?
Where are the people standing in line?

Now Victor's in the theater with Tania. He's sitting between Tania and a man with a mustache. A woman's sitting in front of him. Victor can't see the movie because she's wearing a hat. A man's sitting behind Tania. He's eating potato chips. Tania's angry because she can't hear the movie!

Questions

Where's Victor now?
Who's he with?
Where's he sitting?
Who's sitting in front of him?
Why can't Victor see the movie?
Who's sitting behind him?
What's the man eating?
Why is Tania angry?

This is a scene from the movie. In this scene, a beautiful young woman's lying across the tracks. She's shouting "Help!" because a train's coming along the tracks. It's very near. It's coming around the bend now....

Questions

Where's the woman lying?
What's she shouting?
Why is she shouting?
Is the train near?
Can you see the train?
Where is it?

What's on TV tonight?

Que esta en la T.V. esta noche

Melissa: Hi, David. I'm home.
David: Hi. How are you?
Melissa: I'm tired. How about you?
David: I'm tired too.
Melissa: What time is it?
David: It's a quarter to seven.
Melissa: What's on TV tonight?
David: There's a good program on PBS at a quarter after nine— *Best Animated Movies of the Year.*
Melissa: Yes…and there's a great movie on channel two at eight o'clock, after *Fifty-nine Minutes.*
David: Oh, wait a minute. There's a baseball game on at seven.
Melissa: Oh, I can't watch that. Look! There's ballet on channel thirteen. It's beginning now.
David: But Melissa, it's my favorite team. It's a very important game. It's the World Series!
Melissa: Well, you can watch it on the portable TV in the bedroom.

TELEVISION SCHEDULE

	7:00	7:30	8:00	8:30	9:00	9:30	10:00
2 WCBS (CBS)	59 minutes		Movie: ***What's Happening, Brother? (comedy, 1994) Michelle Spicer, Doug Michaels, Lee Spikes			Election: Special Report	
4 WNBC (NBC)	Baseball: World Series Toronto Blue Jays vs. Atlanta Braves					The Crosby Show	Doctors
5 WNYW (Fox)	Married with Kids	Anna Rose		The Simkins	Lewis Parker Can't Lose	Beverly Streets 91201	Bay Search
7 WABC (ABC)	Empty House	Danger!	Home Videos	Who's the Boss?	Lots of Fun!	Seattle Police Squad	
13 WNET (PBS)	6:45: Royal Canadian Ballet		7:45: Paul Simon: Live in Concert	Art Shots		9:15: Best Animated Movies of the Year	10:15 News

International time

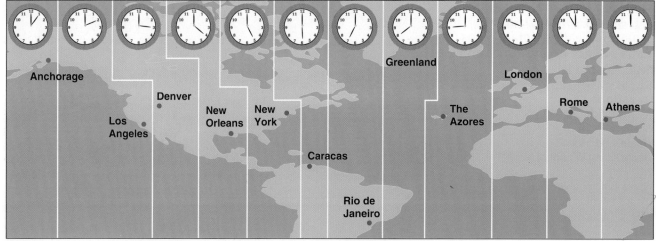

1st	2nd	3rd	4th	5th	6th
It's one o'clock in Anchorage.	Los Angeles	Denver	New Orleans	New York	Caracas

7th	8th	9th	10th	11th	12th
Rio de Janeiro	Greenland	Azores	London	Rome	Athens

Exercise

What time is it?
It's three o'clock.

· · · ·   · · · ·   · · · ·   · · · ·   · · · ·

In prison

Tim: Tomorrow we're going to leave this place!

Fred: Yeah. What are you going to do first?

Tim: Well, I'm going to rent a big car, meet my girlfriend, and take her to an expensive restaurant. We're going to have lobster and caviar. What about you, Fred?

Fred: My wife's going to meet me outside the prison. Then we're going to visit her mother.

Tim: Your mother-in-law? You're kidding!

Fred: No, I'm not. I'm going to work for my wife's mother.

Tim: Really? You're not going to work for your mother-in-law!

Fred: Well, she has a little diner in Chicago.

Tim: What are you going to do there?

Fred: I'm going to be a dishwasher.

Tim: What? Wash dishes? Well, I'm not going to work. I'm going to have a good time!

Fred: You're lucky. I'm going to rob a bank next week.

Tim: Are you crazy? Why?

Fred: Because I'm happy here in prison!

Exercise 1

prison

He's going to leave prison.

Tim

Write sentences with:
1. car
2. girlfriend
3. good time

Exercise 2

car

He isn't going to rent a car.

Fred

Write sentences with:
1. lobster
2. caviar
3. good time

Exercise 3

lobster

They're going to have lobster.

Tim and his girlfriend

Write sentences with:
1. car
2. caviar
3. good time

Exercise 4

caviar

They aren't going to have caviar.

Fred and his wife

Write sentences with:
1. good time
2. lobster
3. car

bride - Novia

A wedding

Un Casamiento

CITY HALL

1

This is an American wedding. The bride and groom are leaving City Hall. The bride is wearing a long white gown and carrying a bouquet of flowers. The groom is wearing a tuxedo and a purple carnation. He's holding her hand. Their friends and relatives are throwing rice. The bride and groom are both smiling because they're very happy.

1. What are the bride and groom doing?
2. What's the bride wearing?
3. What's she carrying?
4. What's the groom wearing?
5. What's he holding?
6. What are their friends doing?
7. Why are the bride and groom smiling?

2

In a few minutes, they're going to get into a white Cadillac and drive to a hotel for the reception. They're going to have dinner, and the bride and groom are going to cut the cake. Some people are going to make speeches, and their parents are going to cry! Then everyone is going to dance.

1. Where are they going to drive to?
2. What are they going to have?
3. What are the bride and groom going to do?
4. What are some people going to do?
5. What are their parents going to do?
6. What's everyone going to do then?

3

Later on, the bride and groom are going to change their clothes. Then they're going to leave the reception and drive to the airport. They're going to fly to Acapulco in Mexico for their honeymoon. They aren't going to tell anyone the address of their hotel!

1. When are the bride and groom going to change their clothes?
2. Where are they going to drive?
3. Where are they going to fly?
4. Who are they going to tell the address of their hotel?

Computadora de citas

Interviewer: Hello. Come in, please.

Mr. Jennson: Good afternoon. My name's Jennson…Magnus Jennson. I'm…uh…looking for a woman friend.

Interviewer: Please sit down, Mr. Jennson. May I ask you some questions?

Mr. Jennson: What about?

Interviewer: Well, about music, for example. Do you like music?

Mr. Jennson: Yes, I do. I like military band music and classical music.

Interviewer: Do you like rock music?

Mr. Jennson: No, I don't! And I don't like jazz.

Interviewer: Uh-huh. OK. Food… Do you like foreign food?

Mr. Jennson: No, I don't. I like meat and potatoes.

Interviewer: OK. How old are you, Mr. Jennson?

Mr. Jennson: What? Listen here, young man. I don't like these personal questions!

Interviewer: Oh, well, uh, can you fill out this form later and mail it to me?

Exercise 1

Look at Magnus Jennson.
Does he like jazz?
Write five questions about him.

Exercise 2

Do you like football?
Write five questions.

Exercise 3

Look at Mary Ellen Turner.
1. She likes cats.
2. She doesn't like dogs.
Write ten sentences about her.

Exercise 4

1. I like movies.
2. I don't like dogs.
Write ten sentences about yourself.

boy

COMPUTER DATING SERVICES, INC.

Last Name: _Jennson_
First Name(s): _Magnus_
Address: _Oslo Farm, Lake Sadness_
Mist County, Minnesota
Age: _65_
Occupation: _Farmer_
Marital Status: ☑ Single ☐ Married
☐ Divorced ☐ Widowed
LIKES:
General: _dogs, fishing_
Colors: _red, white, and blue_
Food: _meat and potatoes_
Hobbies: _golf, chess_
Music: _military bands, classical_
DISLIKES: _rock music, jazz, dancing,_
TV, children
SIGNATURE: _Magnus Jennson_

girl

COMPUTER DATING SERVICES, INC.

Last Name: _Turner_
First Name(s): _Mary Ellen_
Address: _1248 Union Street_
Minneapolis, Minnesota
Age: _57_
Occupation: _Homemaker_
Marital Status: ☐ Single ☐ Married
☐ Divorced ☑ Widowed
viuda
LIKES:
General: _children, TV, cats, dancing_
Colors: _purple, pink, green_
Food: _salads, vegetarian food_
Hobbies: _astrology, reading_
Music: _folk, rock, Top 40, New Age_
DISLIKES: _football, baseball,_
fishing, dogs
SIGNATURE: _Mary E Turner_

Larry: Please marry me, Jacqueline. I want you. I need you. I love you.

Jackie: I'm sorry, Lawrence, but I can't.

Larry: Oh, Jackie, why not?

Jackie: Well, Larry. I like you…. I like you a lot…. But I don't love you.

Larry: But Jackie, love isn't everything.

Jackie: Oh, Larry, you don't understand…. For me, love is everything.

Larry: Do you…love another man, Jackie?

Jackie: Yes, Larry, I do.

Larry: Not…Michael Kennedy?

Jackie: Yes, Michael Kennedy.

Larry: But he doesn't want you. He's engaged!

Jackie: I know.

Larry: But Jackie, Mike isn't a rich man. I can give you everything. What do you want? Clothes? Money? Travel? A house in Palm Beach?

Jackie: No, Larry. I don't want those things. I only want Mike.

Questions

Who wants Jackie?
Does he love her?
Does Jackie like Larry?
Does she like him a lot?
Does she love him?
Does Jackie love another man?
What's his name?
Does Mike want Jackie?
Is he rich?
Is Larry rich?
What can he give Jackie?
Does she want clothes?
Does she want money?
What does she want?

Exercise 1

Who wants Jackie?
Larry wants Jackie.

Who loves Jackie?
Who needs Jackie?
Who wants Mike?
Who loves Mike?

Exercise 2

Who does Larry want?
Larry wants Jackie.

Who does Larry love?
Who does Jackie love?
Who does Jackie want?
Who does Larry need?

Y: Excuse me.
Z: Yes?
Y: Do you have any change?
Z: What do you need?
Y: I need some quarters.
Z: Sure. How many do you want?
Y: Can you change a dollar bill?
Z: Yes, I think so. Here are four quarters.

coins
pennies (1¢)
nickels (5¢)
dimes (10¢)
quarters (25¢)

bills
a dollar bill
a five-dollar bill
a ten-dollar bill
a twenty-dollar bill

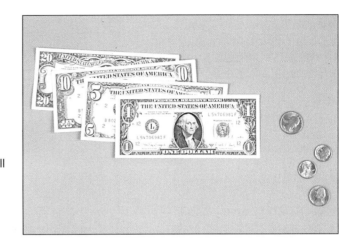

E: Hello.
I: Hello. How can I help you?
E: Could you repair these boots?
I: Sure. What's the problem?
E: They need new heels.
I: No problem. When do you need them?
E: As soon as possible.
I: Is Thursday afternoon OK?
E: Yes. That's great.

Wednesday morning
Saturday afternoon
Friday evening
Monday at noon

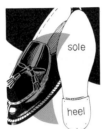

sole

heel

A: Excuse me.
R: Yes?
A: Is there a parking lot near here?
R: Yes, there is.
A: Is it far?
R: No, it's not. Turn right at the first traffic light. It's on the left.
A: Thank you.
R: You're welcome.

post office
bus stop
taxi stand
telephone booth
supermarket

first left
second right

Look at the map and make conversations.

An interview

Arnold Rivera, the TV news reporter, is interviewing Mrs. Cornelia Vandergilt for the program *Real People*.

AR: Well, Mrs. Vandergilt, please tell our viewers about an ordinary day in your life.

CV: Well, I wake up at eight o'clock.

AR: Really? Do you get up then?

CV: No, of course I don't get up at that time. I have breakfast in bed, and I read *The New York Times.*

AR: What time do you get up?

CV: I get up at ten.

AR: What do you do then?

CV: I read my letters and dictate the answers to my secretary.

AR: And then?

CV: At eleven I take a walk with Jimmy.

AR: Jimmy? Who's Jimmy?

CV: Jimmy's my dog.

AR: Oh. What time do you have lunch?

CV: I have lunch at twelve-thirty. I eat alone.

AR: Oh, I see. Well, what do you do after lunch?

CV: I rest until six o'clock.

AR: And at six? What do you do at six?

CV: I get dressed for dinner. I have dinner at seven o'clock.

AR: Yes, well, what do you do after dinner?

CV: I read or watch TV. I take a bath at nine-thirty. And I go to bed at ten.

AR: You certainly have a busy and interesting life, Mrs. Vandergilt. Thank you.

CV: You're welcome.

Questions

Who's interviewing Mrs. Cornelia Vandergilt?
Does she wake up at nine o'clock?
Ask, "What time?"
Does she have breakfast in the kitchen?
Ask, "Where?"
Does she read the *Los Angeles Times?*
Ask, "What?"
Does she read her letters?
Does she dictate the answers to her husband?

Does she take a walk with her secretary?
Ask, "Who with?"
Does she have lunch at 12?
Ask, "What time?"
What does she do until six?
What does she do at six?
Does she have dinner at eight?
Ask, "What time?"
Does she go to bed at nine-thirty?
Ask, "What time?"

Exercise

a. *She reads* The New York Times.
b. *She doesn't read* the Los Angeles Times.
c. *Does she read* Time magazine?

a. She walks with her dog.
b. . . . with her secretary.
c. . . . with her husband?

a. She eats lunch alone.
b. . . . with Jimmy.
c. . . . with her husband?

1. Mac's a truck driver.
2. He's twenty-five years old.
3. He works five days a week.
4. He gets up at six o'clock every day.
5. He eats an enormous breakfast.
6. He drinks two cups of coffee.
7. Then he kisses his wife good-bye.
8. He leaves for work at six-thirty.
9. He has lunch at a hamburger place.
10. He comes home at five o'clock.
11. He has dinner and watches TV.
12. He goes to bed at ten o'clock.

Questions

1. What does Mac do?
2. How old is he?
3. How many days a week does he work?
4. What time does he get up?
5. What does he eat for breakfast?
6. What does he drink?
7. What does he do after breakfast?
8. What time does he leave for work?
9. Where does he have lunch?
10. What time does he come home?
11. What does he do in the evening?
12. What time does he go to bed?

Exercise

Now ask (and answer) questions about these people:

1. architect
2. 35
3. 5 days a week
4. 7:30
5. nothing
6. orange juice
7. daughter
8. the office/9:15
9. in a coffee shop
10. home/6:00
11. go out with friends
12. midnight

1. students
2. 12
3. go to school/5 days a week
4. 7:00
5. cereal
6. milk
7. mother
8. school/8:30
9. in the cafeteria
10. home/4:00
11. watch TV
12. nine o'clock

1. homemaker
2. 31
3. not/work/5 days a week
4. 5:30
5. toast
6. tea
7. wife (she goes to work)
8. supermarket/9:00
9. at home
10. wife/comes home/5:30
11. play with their kids
12. ten-thirty

What's My Job?

Host: Good evening, ladies and gentlemen. Welcome to *What's My Job?* We have three famous people here—Dr. K. Walter Eisenstein, the scientist; Bonita Moreno, the movie star; and Rude E. Mallet, the rock star. They're going to ask the questions. Now here's our first contestant. OK, Dr. Eisenstein…

Dr. Eisenstein: Umm, do you work outside?

Contestant: No, I don't.

Dr. Eisenstein: I see. Do you work in an office?

Contestant: Well, yes. Yes, I do.

Dr. Eisenstein: Do you wear a uniform?

Contestant: No, I don't.

Host: Next, Bonita Moreno.

Ms. Moreno: Oh, is your job important?

Contestant: Yes, it is.

Ms. Moreno: Do you get a big salary?

Contestant: Yes, I do.

Ms. Moreno: Do you have any special diplomas?

Contestant: Yes, I do.

Host: Thank you, Bonita. Now, Rude E. Mallet.

Mr. Mallet: What's happening…? Do you work with your hands?

Contestant: Yes, I do.

Mr. Mallet: Do you work on weekends?

Contestant: No, I don't.

Mr. Mallet: Do you travel in your work?

Contestant: No, I don't.

Host: That's the ninth question! Now you can ask one last question.

Ms. Moreno: Are you a doctor?

Contestant: No, I'm not. I'm a dentist.

Electrician

Teacher

Artist

Secretary

Ballet dancer

Bank manager

Lemon Computers, Inc., always has an end-of-the-year party for its workers. They usually have dinner and then they dance. This year they're doing something different. They're having a karaoke party.

Travis: Come on, Brittany. Sing us a song!

Brittany: No way!

Travis: Why not?

Brittany: I never sing in public!

Travis: But you *can* sing.

Brittany: Well, I often sing in the car. But that's different. I'm on my own then.

Travis: Only in the car?

Brittany: Well, I occasionally sing in the shower. But everybody sometimes sings in the shower.

Travis: Well, there you go. You *can* sing.

Brittany: Travis, I really don't want to.

Travis: What's your favorite song?

Brittany: I don't know. I hardly ever listen to rock music. I usually listen to opera.

Travis: They don't have opera, Brittany. You know that. Come on! Think of a song.

Brittany: Oh, all right!

Travis: Ladies and gentlemen! Our next singer is Brittany Young from the Sales Division…

Brittany: *You always ask me questions. I never tell you lies…*

1. Every morning he brushes his teeth. He always brushes his teeth in the morning.
2. She gets up at 7 o'clock from Monday to Saturday, but on Sunday she gets up at 11 o'clock. She usually gets up at 7 o'clock.
3. They like movies. They see all the new movies. They often go to the movies.
4. She has a radio and a TV. She sometimes listens to the radio, and she sometimes watches TV.
5. Her brother lives in Texas. She doesn't. She sees him four or five times every year. She occasionally sees him.

6. He doesn't usually sing, but once a year, at his company's end-of-the-year party, he sings a song. He hardly ever sings in public.
7. She doesn't like coffee. She never drinks coffee.

Exercise 1

He/sometimes/football.
He sometimes *plays* football.

1. They/often/potatoes.
2. She/usually/a skirt.
3. I/never/a hat.
4. He/occasionally/TV.
5. We/hardly ever/tea.
6. You/never/baseball.

Exercise 2

coffee
I sometimes drink coffee.
or
I never drink coffee.
or
I hardly ever drink coffee.

Now write one true sentence for each:

1. coffee
2. TV
3. golf
4. spaghetti
5. cola
6. caviar
7. a newspaper
8. the movies
9. new clothes
10. a tie
11. homework
12. rock music

A questionnaire

Arthur McNair works for a market research company in San Francisco. He's asking people about their free time:

AM: Excuse me, ma'am.
Janet Ross: Yes?
AM: I'm from Market Research, Inc. May I ask you some questions?
JR: Uh, yes, all right.
AM: Thank you. First, what time do you usually get home from work?
JR: Um, I usually get home about six o'clock.
AM: When do you usually have dinner?
JR: I usually eat about seven, but I sometimes eat at eight or nine. My husband works too!

AM: What do you usually do after dinner?
JR: Well, I sometimes go out, but I usually stay home and read or watch TV.
AM: How often do you go out?
JR: Oh, not often…about once or twice a week.
AM: Do you often see your friends?
JR: Yes, I do. Pretty often. I sometimes visit them, and they sometimes visit me.
AM: Do you ever go to the movies?
JR: Oh, yes.
AM: How often?
JR: Well, occasionally…. I like horror movies—*Frankenstein* or *Dracula.*

AM: What about the theater? Do you ever go to the theater?
JR: Yes, I do, but not often. In fact, I hardly ever go to the theater.
AM: Do you ever go to the ballet?
JR: No, never. I don't like ballet.
AM: Well, thank you, Ms. Ross.
JR: May I ask you a question?
AM: Yes?
JR: What do you do in *your* spare time?
AM: I ask questions, Ms. Ross. I never answer them.
JR: Oh!

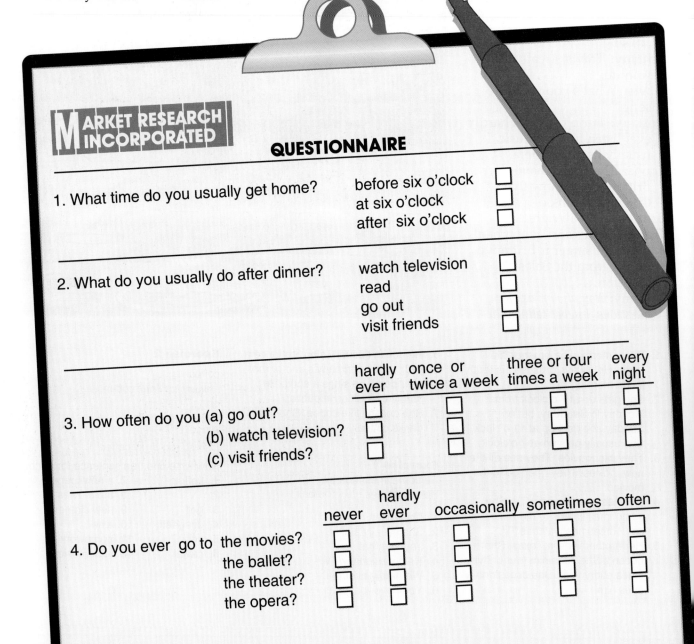

Hello. My name's Chuck Seeger. I'm a pilot for Global Airlines. I fly 747s. I'm not working today; I'm playing golf. It's my favorite sport.

Questions
What's his name?
What does he do?
What does he fly?
What's he doing now?
What's his favorite sport?

This woman's a violinist. Her name's Michiko. She plays the violin in the Boston Symphony Orchestra. She isn't playing the violin right now. She's dancing with her boyfriend.

Questions
What's her name?
What does she do?
Who's she with right now?
What are they doing?

This is a picture of Joan and Dave. They teach English at a language school in San Francisco. They aren't teaching right now. They're in a restaurant. They're talking about their students.

Questions
Who are they?
What do they do?
Are they teaching right now?
Where are they?
What are they doing?

This is Cynthia Graham. She dances for the New York City Ballet. She isn't dancing right now. She's taking a bath in her hotel room. Later she's going to dance at the White House for the president and his guests.

Questions
What's her name?
What does she do?
Is she dancing right now?
What's she doing?
What's she going to do later?

Exercise

Reggie Johnson, baseball player
Example:
a. *What does he do? He plays baseball.*
b. *What's he doing right now? He's sleeping.*

Kathleen and
Kate, singers
a. • • • •.
• • • •.
b. • • • •.
• • • •.

Lucy Dooley,
artist
a. • • • •.
• • • •.
b. • • • •.
• • • •.

There's a baseball game on TV today. The New York Rebels are playing the Chicago Blue Socks. They are both good teams. They usually play well. But today the Rebels are playing very well, and the Blue Socks are playing badly.

Questions
Which teams are playing?
Are they good teams?
Do they usually play well or badly?
How are the Rebels playing today?
How are the Blue Socks playing?

William Zanzinger often has accidents. This is his fourth accident this year. He's a bad driver because he's a fast and careless driver. He drives fast, carelessly, and badly.

Questions
Does William often have accidents?
Is this his first accident this year?
Is he a good or bad driver?
Does he drive well or badly?
Is he a fast or slow driver?
Does he drive carefully or carelessly?

John Gonzalez is an excellent driver. He always drives slowly, carefully, and well. All his friends say, "John's a good driver! He's very careful."

Questions
Is John a good driver or a bad driver?
Does he drive well or badly?
Is he a fast driver or a slow driver?
Does he drive carefully or carelessly?

Susan Yamakawa works very hard. She's a fast worker. Her boss often says, "Ms. Yamakawa works hard eight hours a day. She's a hard worker and a good employee."

Questions
Is Susan a hard worker or a lazy worker?
Does she work hard or lazily?
Is she a fast or a slow worker?
Does she work fast or slowly?

Exercise

Kevin's a good player.
How does he play?
He plays well.

1. You're a bad swimmer.
2. She's a careful driver.
3. John's a slow learner.
4. They're hard workers.
5. He's a fast walker.

Look at this:

+ -ly	-y to -ily	irregular/no change
bad/badly	happy/happily	good/well
slow/slowly	busy/busily	fast/fast
careful/carefully	noisy/noisily	hard/hard
careless/carelessly		

A: What are you doing this weekend?
B: I'm going out of town.
A: Oh? Where are you going?
B: I'm going to Cape Cod.
A: For how long?
B: Just for two days.

this weekend
on Saturday
tomorrow
next week
on Thanksgiving

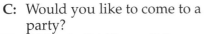

C: Would you like to come to a party?
D: Well, uh, I'd like to. When is it?
C: Saturday night.
D: Oh, sorry. I'm busy on Saturday.
C: What are you doing?
D: Uh…I'm doing my homework.
C: Your homework?
D: That's right.
C: Well, maybe some other time.
D: Right. Uh, thanks anyway.

party
dance
rock concert
baseball game

Saturday
Sunday
Monday
Tuesday
Wednesday
Thursday
Friday

E: Would you like to dance?
F: OK.
E: Do you come here often?
F: Sometimes.
E: Do you live near here?
F: No, I don't.
E: Where do you work?
F: In a bank.
E: Do you like it?
F: It's OK.

sometimes
once a week
twice a week
every night
occasionally

Where do you work?
Where do you go to
  school?
Where do you
  study?

Make conversations. Go around the class and ask three students these questions. Check the boxes after each student's answer (✓ = yes, x = no).

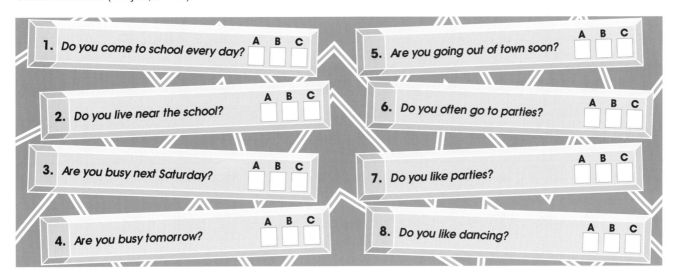

1. Do you come to school every day? A B C
2. Do you live near the school? A B C
3. Are you busy next Saturday? A B C
4. Are you busy tomorrow? A B C
5. Are you going out of town soon? A B C
6. Do you often go to parties? A B C
7. Do you like parties? A B C
8. Do you like dancing? A B C

Lost in Niagara Falls

Look at the map. Put *A*, *B*, *C*, or *D* next to the conversations.

☐ **Bill:** Excuse me, I'm looking for the Skylon Tower.
Woman: Pardon me?
Bill: I'm looking for the Skylon Tower.
Woman: It's right behind you. You're standing right in front of it.

☐ **Bill:** Where can I find the boat trip to the Falls?
Man: Ah, you want the *Maid of the Mists* Plaza. Walk along this street—it's the Niagara Parkway. Stay near the river; the road goes around to the right. The entrance to the boat trips is just around the bend on your right. You can't miss it.
Bill: Sorry. Could you repeat that?

☐ **Bill:** Pardon me. How do I get to the United States?
Woman: Just go straight ahead. Go across the Rainbow Bridge and you're there! This side's Canada, that side's the U.S.A.

☐ **Bill:** Which are the Canadian Falls?
Man: They're on our right. The Horseshoe Falls is another name for the Canadian Falls.

Bill: So, the American Falls are across the river on our left.
Man: That's correct.

Exercise

You are at C. Give another student directions to:
1. The Minolta Tower
2. The Greenhouse
3. The Rainbow Bridge
4. Table Rock House

A: AMC Movie Theater. How can I help you?

B: I'd like two tickets for *Aladdin*, please.

A: For when?

B: Saturday at four o'clock.

A: December 26th, four o'clock. That's $9. How would you like to pay?

B: Visa. Card number 9999 8160 2277 4538.

A: And what's your name?

B: Lee. William Lee.

A: And the expiration date on the card?

B: July of next year.

C: Are you a student here?

D: Yes. It's my first day.

C: What are you studying?

D: E.S.L.

C: Oh, where are you from?

D: São Paulo in Brazil.

C: Are you a student in Brazil?

D: No, I'm not. I work for an airline.

C: Oh, really? Which one?

D: Varig. Do you know it?

E: Hello. I'd like a membership card for the Recreation Center.

F: The Center is for the Brentwood area only.

E: Yes, I know.

F: Do you live, work, or go to school in the area?

E: I go to school here.

F: Do you have a student ID?

E: It's right here. I'm a student at Brentwood College.

F: OK. Can you complete this form? I also need a passport photograph and $20.

E: Is there a student discount?

F: Yes. There's a discount of twenty-five percent. Twenty dollars is the discount price.

Exercise 1

Interview another student and complete the form.

Exercise 2

Interview a different student. Ask about the answers on his or her form, e.g.:

What's (her) name?

Where does (she) live?

Tuesday, 5/23
6:30 PM
Thursday, 8/17
11:45 AM
Sunday, 1/30
2:15 PM
Wednesday, 9/13
5:00 PM

São Paulo, Brazil, Varig
Osaka, Japan, All Nippon Airways
Seoul, Korea, Korean Air
Monterrey, Mexico, AeroMexico

(go to school) -
student ID
James Polk High School
The State University

(live) - driver's license
on 56th Street
in South Brentwood

(work) - employee ID
for Lemon Computers
at the library

Brentwood Recreation Center

Application for Center Membership

Please complete the form clearly in CAPITAL LETTERS in ink.

Last Name: _____

First Name: _____ Middle Initial: _____

Title: (Mr./Mrs./Miss/Ms./Other) _____

Date of Birth: _____

Address: _____

Signature: _____ Date: _____

Where were you?

Princess Amelia of Silvania is on a skiing trip to Aspen, Colorado. Princess Amelia employs three security guards. They're outside her hotel now. They're talking to a photographer. The Princess has a lot of problems with photographers!

Guard: OK. Don't move! What's your name, bud?
Justin: Hanson. Justin Hanson. I work for *The National Questioner.*
Guard: Right! You were here yesterday.
Justin: No, I wasn't.
Guard: Yes, you were. You were here yesterday afternoon.
Justin: I wasn't! I was in Denver yesterday.
Guard: Yeah? What about Saturday? Where were you on Saturday?
Justin: Uh…what time?
Guard: Two o'clock. Where were you at two o'clock?
Justin: Uh, I was here, on the ski slope.
Guard: Right! And where were you on January 12th?
Justin: I can't remember.
Guard: It was a Wednesday.
Justin: Oh, really? No, I can't remember.
Guard: I can. You were in New York. Outside Princess Amelia's hotel. And where were you at seven o'clock this evening?
Justin: I'm not answering any more questions.
Guard: Yes, you are, bud. You were outside the swimming pool. With your camera. And the Princess was in the pool.
Justin: OK. But there wasn't any film in my camera.
Guard: Yeah, right. OK, open your camera!

Questions

Where were you at	one o'clock? five after two? ten after three? a quarter after four? five-thirty? twenty to seven?	I was at	home. school. work. the movies. the supermarket. the bank.

Questions

When were you in	New York? Europe? Mexico? Brazil? Colombia? California? Korea? Japan?	I was there in	January. February. March. April. May. June. July. August. September. October. November. December.

Exercise 1

Look at this example:
I/here/two o'clock
I was here at two o'clock.
1. He/Italy/July
2. They/home/Sunday
3. You/here/one o'clock
4. She/school/yesterday
5. It/cold/January
6. We/Rio/Wednesday

Exercise 2

Look at this example:
You/New York/February?
Were you in New York in February?
1. he/Oregon/November?
2. it/hot/June?
3. they/at work/five-thirty?
4. she/home/Thursday?
5. you/there/four o'clock?
6. they/China/December?

Diane: Hi, Joe. Where were you last month?

Joe: Oh, hi, Diane. I was on vacation.

Diane: Really? But you were on vacation in January.

Joe: Yes, I was in Colorado in January.

Diane: Where were you last month?

Joe: I was in Florida.

Diane: Florida? What was it like?

Joe: Fantastic! The weather was beautiful and the ocean was very warm.

Diane: What was the hotel like?

Joe: Excellent! There was a swimming pool and a private beach. And there were three restaurants.

Diane: What were the people like?

Joe: They were very friendly.

Diane: Was Suzanne with you?

Joe: Yes. She loves the sun.

Diane: What about your children? Were they with you?

Joe: No, they weren't. They were with their grandparents in Chicago.

The Gulf Beach Club Hotel

• Three restaurants
• Private beach
• Swimming pool
• Four tennis courts
• Golf course
• Children's pool
• Beach Shop
• Two game rooms
• Health club

Exercise 1

There was a swimming pool.
There were three restaurants.

Now you write six other sentences.

Exercise 2

weather
What was the weather like?

restaurants
What were the restaurants like?
1. service
2. stores
3. food
4. beaches
5. hotel
6. people

Return from space

Phil Strongarm, the astronaut, is talking about his journey to the moon. Opel Winford, the TV personality, is interviewing Phil.

Opel: Well, Phil, welcome back to Earth.

Phil: Thanks, ma'am. Uh, Ms. Winford…I mean, Opel.

Opel: Did you have any problems on the trip into space?

Phil: We didn't have any serious problems, but it certainly wasn't a picnic.

Opel: What do you mean?

Phil: We didn't have a bath or shave for two weeks.

Opel: Oh, really?

Phil: Yes. It wasn't very comfortable.

Opel: What about food? Was that a problem?

Phil: Well, we didn't have any normal food.

Opel: What did you have?

Phil: We had some food tablets and other kinds of food in tubes.

Opel: Are you going to the moon again, Phil?

Phil: I hope so, um, Opel. It was uncomfortable and difficult…but it was wonderful.

Questions

Who's Phil Strongarm?
What's Phil talking about?
Who's interviewing him?
Was it comfortable or uncomfortable?
Did they have any normal food?
What did they have?
Is Phil going to the moon again?
Was it wonderful?

Exercise 1

I/breakfast/eight o'clock
I had breakfast at eight o'clock.
1. You/coffee/eleven o'clock
2. He/lunch/12:30
3. She/a snack/3:30
4. They/dinner/eight o'clock
5. We/supper/nine o'clock

Exercise 2

they/a vacation/last year?
Did they have a vacation last year?
1. he/a haircut/last week?
2. you/a good time/last night?
3. she/a birthday/last month?
4. they/a party/last weekend?
5. you/an appointment/this morning?

Exercise 3

We/a lesson/Sunday
We didn't have a lesson on Sunday.
1. He/a date/Saturday
2. She/a haircut/Monday
3. We/a drink/Tuesday
4. I/a party/Thursday
5. He/a good time/Friday

Did you get everything?

Ron Carter goes downtown every Saturday. He went downtown last Saturday. He usually plays pool with his friends. He played pool last Saturday afternoon. After he leaves the pool hall, he usually goes to the supermarket and gets the food for the week. He got the food last Saturday. He usually comes home by bus. But last Saturday he came home by taxi.

Questions

Does he usually go downtown on Saturday?
What about last Saturday?
Does he meet his friends sometimes?
What about last Saturday?
Does he usually play pool?
What about last Saturday?
Does he usually buy food for the whole week?
What about last Saturday?
Does he usually come home by bus?
What about last Saturday?

Sue: Ron, is that you?
Ron: Yes, Sue. I'm back.
Sue: Did you come home by taxi?
Ron: Yes, I did. The bags were very heavy.
Sue: Did you get everything?
Ron: Yes. I got…well, almost everything.
Sue: Almost everything?
Ron: Well, I went to the butcher, but they didn't have any steak.
Sue: They didn't have any steak?
Ron: No, so I got some hamburgers.
Sue: Did you go to the bakery?
Ron: Yes, but I didn't get any bread.
Sue: You didn't get any bread?
Ron: Well, no, they didn't have any bread. But they had some rolls, so I got some rolls.
Sue: How many rolls did you get?
Ron: Uh, I can't remember.
Sue: Ron?
Ron: Yes?
Sue: What time did you go to the store?
Ron: Uh…I went at five o'clock. The shelves were empty!

Exercise 1

They had some hamburgers.
They didn't have any steak.
Did they have any chicken?

1. He came home by taxi.
   • • • by car.
   • • • by bus?
2. He went to the butcher.
   • • • drugstore.
   • • • bakery?
3. He got some rolls.
   • • • bread.
   • • • hamburgers?

Exercise 2

Answer these questions with *Yes, I did* or *No, I didn't.*

1. Did you go downtown last Saturday? • • • •
2. Did you get anything? • • • •
3. Did you come home by bus?
   • • • •

Jane: Hello, Gloria.
Gloria: Hi, Jane. Did you enjoy lunch?
Jane: Yes, I did. Did you finish those reports?
Gloria: Yes, I typed them. They're on your desk.
Jane: Did you photocopy them?
Gloria: Yes, I photocopied everything. And I mailed the letters too.
Jane: Good. Thank you.
Gloria: You're welcome. Oh, Mr. Thompson was here.
Jane: Mr. Thompson? Did he call for an appointment first?
Gloria: No, he didn't.
Jane: What time did he arrive?
Gloria: About two o'clock. But he only waited about five minutes.
Jane: That's strange. What did he want?
Gloria: He probably wanted some free advice.
Jane: Did anybody telephone?
Gloria: No, nobody.
Jane: Oh, no!
Gloria: What's the matter?
Jane: You mailed the letters….
Gloria: Yes, of course.
Jane: But I didn't sign them!
Gloria: I signed them… with my name.
Jane: *Phew!* Thank you, Gloria. That was great.

Exercise

Who typed the reports?
Gloria *typed the reports.*
Jane *didn't type the reports.*
Did Mr. Thompson *type the reports?*

1. Who mailed the letters?
   Gloria . . . .
   Jane . . . .
   . . . Mr. Thompson . . . ?

2. Who arrived at 2 PM?
   Mr. Thompson . . . .
   Jane . . . .
   . . . Gloria . . . ?

3. Who wanted advice?
   Mr. Thompson . . . .
   Gloria . . . .
   . . . Jane . . . ?

The Legend of Willy the Kid

WILLY THE KID ARRIVED IN DODGE CITY ONE EVENING.

HE WALKED INTO THE SALOON, AND LOOKED SLOWLY AROUND THE ROOM.

EVERYBODY WAS AFRAID. WILLY HAD TWO GUNS.

THE SHERIFF WAS IN HIS OFFICE. HE WAS ASLEEP.

WILLY THE KID'S IN TOWN.

THE BARKEEPER RUSHED INTO THE SHERIFF'S OFFICE.

THE SHERIFF HURRIED TO THE SALOON.

GIVE ME YOUR GUNS, WILLY.

THIS TOWN IS TOO SMALL FOR BOTH OF US.

THE SHERIFF SHOUTED TO WILLY.

WILLY REPLIED CALMLY.

THEY WALKED INTO THE STREET. THE SHERIFF WAITED. WILLY MOVED HIS HAND TOWARD HIS GUN...

THE SHERIFF PULLED OUT HIS GUN. HE FIRED TWICE.

THE FIRST BULLET MISSED WILLY. THE SECOND KILLED HIM.

TWO COWBOYS CARRIED WILLY AWAY. THAT WAS THE END OF WILLY THE KID.

Exercise

1. He walked into the saloon.
   He didn't . . . into the office.
   Did he . . . into the bank?
2. They carried Willy away.
   They . . . carry the sheriff away.
   . . . they carry the barkeeper away?

1 Maria's a student at Yale University. She studies Spanish, and she goes to Mexico every summer. She sees interesting places, lies in the sun, and eats a lot of Mexican food. She always flies to Mexico with AeroMexico.

Questions
1. Is Maria a student?
2. Does she study French?
3. Ask, "What?"
4. Does she go to Brazil every summer?
5. Ask, "Where?"
6. What does she do in Mexico?
7. How does she fly there?

2 Professor Hopkins teaches Spanish at Yale University. He's Maria's teacher. He went to India last summer. He saw the Taj Mahal and rode on an elephant. He wrote postcards to all his friends. He flew with Air–India.

Questions
1. What does Professor Hopkins teach?
2. Where did he go last summer?
3. What did he see?
4. What did he ride on?
5. Who did he write to?
6. Did he fly with Air–India or US Air?

3 Maria's parents went to Italy last year. They toured the country by bus. They saw a lot of interesting places. They ate spaghetti in Rome, drank coffee in Venice, and took a lot of photographs. The sun shone every day. They flew to Italy with Alitalia.

Questions
1. Where did Maria's parents go?
2. How did they tour the country?
3. What did they eat?
4. What did they drink?
5. How many photographs did they take?
6. What was the weather like?
7. Did they go to Italy by plane or by boat?

4 Paulo's from Brazil. He traveled around the United States last summer. He stayed there for a month. Of course he ate hamburgers and drank soda. He met a lot of interesting people. He bought a lot of souvenirs and took them back to Brazil. He flew there with Varig.

Questions
1. What did Paulo do last summer?
2. How long did he stay?
3. What did he eat?
4. What did he drink?
5. Who did he meet?
6. What did he buy?
7. Where did he take his souvenirs?
8. Did he fly with Varig or with United Airlines?

Exercise

a. Anne/go/Spain   a. Anne *went* to Spain.

b. He/not/Spain   b. He *didn't go* to Spain.

c. you/Spain?   c. *Did you go* to Spain?

a. They/eat/spaghetti
b. He/not/spaghetti
c. you/spaghetti?

a. They/drink/coffee
b. She/not/coffee
c. you/coffee?

a. He/see/Taj Mahal
b. She/not/Taj Mahal
c. you/Taj Mahal?

a. He/buy/CDs
b. They/not/CDs
c. you/CDs?

Look at this:

have	had	fly	flew
come	came	shine	shone
go	went	meet	met
get	got	write	wrote
see	saw	ride	rode
eat	ate	buy	bought
drink	drank	bring	brought
take	took		

Survivors

Bill Craig and Chris Alonso are test pilots. Last year their plane crashed in the Pacific Ocean. They were in a rubber lifeboat for four weeks.
They didn't have much water, and they didn't have many things to eat. They had a few bananas and a little apple juice from their plane. They caught a lot of fish.
They had only a little chocolate. They had only a few crackers and a few apples. They lost a lot of weight.

After four weeks they were lucky. They saw a ship and it rescued them. They wrote a book about their experience. It's called *Survivors.*

Questions
What are their names?
What do they do?
Did their plane crash?
Ask, "When?"
Ask, "Where?"
How many weeks were they in a lifeboat?
How much water did they have?
Did they have many bananas?
Did they have much apple juice?
Did they catch any fish?
Ask, "How many?"
How much chocolate did they have?
How many crackers did they have?
How many apples did they have?
What happened after four weeks?
What did they write?

Exercise 1

chocolate

A: Did they have any chocolate?
B: Yes, they did. But they didn't have much.

A: How much chocolate did they have?
B: They had only a little.

water

gas

apple juice

Exercise 2

matches

A: Did they have any matches?
B: Yes, they did. But they didn't have many.

A: How many matches did they have?
B: They had only a few.

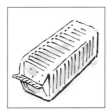

crackers

apples

bananas

Exercise 3

He doesn't have *much* money.
He has only *a little* money.
She doesn't have *many* dollars.
She has only *a few* dollars.
1. He doesn't have . . . friends.
2. He has only . . . friends.

3. He doesn't have . . . water.
4. He has only . . . water.
5. She didn't have . . . Swiss francs.
6. She had only . . . French francs.
7. There isn't . . . gas.
8. We have only . . . gas.

Misha Botnick is the director of *Fifth Avenue*. It's the morning after the first performance. He's speaking to the performers.

Misha: Well, guys, I worked hard. You worked hard. We all worked hard…. What happened last night?!…YOU WERE TERRIBLE! The show was terrible! Whitney!

Whitney: Yes, Mr. Botnick?

Misha: Look, Whitney. You're a good singer. You usually sing well.

Whitney: Thank you, Mr. Botnick.

Misha: But last night you sang badly, Whitney. What happened?

Whitney: I don't know, Mr. Botnick…I sang the last song well.

Misha: "I sang the last song well." You forgot the words, Whitney!

Misha: Why are you laughing, Jason?

Jason: Sorry, Mr. Botnick.

Misha: Jason, you're famous. You're a great dancer. I saw you dance in Boston. You danced very well. You're the star of this show.

Jason: I'm sorry about last night, Mr. Botnick. I had one or two problems….

Misha: One or two! First you lost your shoe. Then you danced badly in the love scene….

Jason: I only had one shoe, Mr. Botnick.

Misha: And finally, Jason, finally…you fell into the orchestra pit.

Questions
Who is Misha Botnick?
What does Whitney do?
Is she a good singer or a bad singer?
How does Whitney usually sing?
How did she sing last night?

What does Jason do?
How does he usually dance?
How did he dance last night?
How many problems did Jason have?
What were the problems?

Exercise 1
He's a good dancer.
He usually dances well.

1. They're beautiful dancers.
2. She's a careless writer.
3. He's a hard worker.
4. He's a bad football player.
5. They're good drivers.

Exercise 2
He usually dances well, *but yesterday he danced badly.*

1. She usually writes carefully, • • • .
2. She usually types slowly, • • • .
3. They usually sing badly, • • • .
4. He usually works fast, • • • .
5. He usually answers carelessly, • • • .

G: Hi, there. I'm David and I'm your waiter for today. Are you enjoying your vacation?
H: Yes, thanks.
G: Is this your first day in Orlando?
G: No, we came here two days ago.
H: Where are you from?
G: Canada…. We're from Toronto.
H: Did you go to a theme park yesterday?
G: Yes. We went to Universal Studios.
H: Did you have a good time?
G: Yes, thank you.
H: Great! Now, what can I get you for breakfast?

two days ago
last week
three days ago
five days ago

Universal Studios
Disney-MGM Studios
  Theme Park
Magic Kingdom®
  Park
EPCOT® Center

I: What did you do last weekend?
J: I went to Tampa.
I: Really? How did you go?
J: I went by car.
I: How long did it take?
J: It took about two hours.
I: Did you have a good time?
J: Yeah, great.

last weekend
yesterday
last Saturday
last night

car
taxi
bus
train

K: Excuse me. I left my glasses here this morning.
L: Where did you leave them?
K: Over there. I was at the table by the window.
L: Well, you're lucky. The waiter found them about an hour ago.
K: Thank goodness! I was really worried.
L: There you go. He gave them to me a few minutes ago.
K: Yes. Those are mine. They're new. I lost my last pair.

my glasses
some packages
an umbrella
some shopping bags
my camera

about an hour ago
a few minutes ago
half an hour ago
15 minutes ago
a short time ago

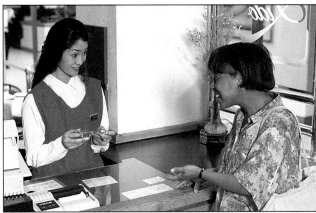

Exercise 1

A: Where did you go yesterday?
B: I went to Tampa. There was a lot of traffic.
A: How long did it take?/How far is it?
B: It took about three hours./It's about 90 miles.
A: How long does it usually take?
B: About two hours.

Make more conversations with the map.

Exercise 2

Ask and answer.
1. How did you come to school today?
2. How long did it take?
3. What did you do last weekend?
4. What did you do yesterday evening?
5. Where were you (an hour) ago?
6. Where were you (two years) ago?

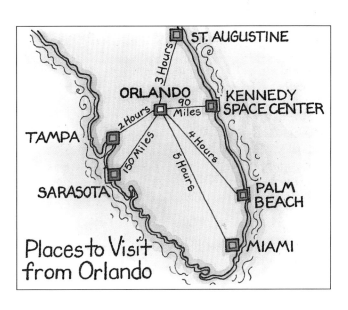

Places to Visit from Orlando

The Six O'Clock News

Good evening. This is the *Six O'Clock News* from Washington with J. C. Kennedy and Warren Wolf.

Last night there was an earthquake in Mandanga. The earthquake destroyed the Central Bank. Many buildings fell down. The Mandangan army is in the capital. They are helping survivors. The Red Cross sent planes with food and medicine to the area this morning.

Questions
What happened in Mandanga?
Ask, "When?"
Did the earthquake destroy the airport?
Ask, "What?"
How many buildings fell down?
Where is the army?
What are they doing?
What did the Red Cross do?
Ask, "When?"

The Virginia police are looking for two climbers in the Blue Ridge Mountains. The climbers left yesterday morning to climb Mount Blue. It began to snow heavily yesterday afternoon. The police sent out a search party last night. They spent the night on the mountain, but they didn't find the climbers.

Questions
How many climbers are the police looking for?
Ask, "Where?"
When did they leave?
What did they want to climb?
Did it rain or did it snow?
Who sent out a search party?
Ask, "When?"
Did they spend the night in a hotel?
Ask, "Where?"
Did they find the climbers?

Yesterday, Washington, D.C. mayor, Nancy Burns, opened a new rehabilitation center in the D.C. Hospital. She met all the doctors and nurses, and spoke to the first patients. Mrs. Burns does a lot of work with the disabled.

Questions
Who opened a new rehabilitation center?
Ask, "When?"
Ask, "Where?"
Who did she meet?
Who did she speak to?
Who does she do a lot of work with?

And that's the news for tonight. Now, over to Jasmine Gonzalez for the weather report....

January 28, 1962 Janine was born in Manchester, England, at 3:35 AM. Her mother died a few days later.

March 1962 Mr. and Mrs. Swift adopted Janine.

1965 The Swift family emigrated to the U.S.A.

1968 Janine started school in San Francisco. Everyone called her Jan.

1974 Jan went into the hospital. They removed her appendix.

1981 Jan graduated from high school. She went to college. She majored in nursing.

1984 Jan started work at a hospital in Oakland.

1986 Jan became a paramedic. She also drove an ambulance.

1988 Jan married Ricardo (Ricky), an electrical engineer. Ricky's parents were from Cuba.

1989 Jan's daughter, Rebecca, was born.

1991 Jan's son, James, was born.

1993 Jan visited England on vacation.

Janine's search

Janine went to the hospital in Manchester and asked about her family. She found some interesting news! She was a twin. She had a twin sister! A TV company heard about Janine's story. They investigated for her. Janine's sister lived in Australia. They both had long dark hair. They both liked classical music. In fact, everything about them was almost the same.

Questions

Ask a partner these questions and find out the facts about Janine's sister's life. (The answers are on the bottom of the page.)

What's her sister's name?
What time was she born?
Who adopted her?
When did they emigrate to Australia?
When did she start school?
Where did she start school?
Did she go into the hospital?
Ask, "When?"

What happened?
When did she graduate from high school?
What did she do then?
What happened in 1986?
When did she get married?
Who did she marry?
Where were his parents from?
How many children does she have?
When were they born?
What are their names?
Where did the TV company find her?

Dinner with a star

Harriet Dormer won a magazine contest. The prize was dinner in Hollywood with a movie star. She's having dinner with Kevin Costley, the actor.

Harriet: Why, Mr. Costley, this is a change. I don't usually eat in restaurants, you know.

Kevin: Well, you're eating in a restaurant tonight. Do you like it?

Harriet: Ooh, yes, Mr. Costley. It's wonderful.

Kevin: Please don't call me Mr. Costley. My friends always call me Kevin.

Harriet: All right…Kevin. And we're having filet mignon. I normally have franks and beans on Mondays. You see, my husband doesn't like restaurants.

Kevin: Tell me about your husband. What's he doing now?

Harriet: He's just over there. He's recording a video for me. Could you wave to him, Mr. Cos…I mean, Kevin?

Kevin: Sure. What's his name?

Harriet: Andrew.

Kevin: Hello, there, Andy! Good to see you! How's it going?

Harriet: Thank you.

Kevin: Would you like a drink? Champagne, maybe?

Harriet: Oh, I never drink alcohol. A diet soda, please.

Kevin: Fine. I'd like a diet soda, too. I'm filming tonight.

Harriet: Uh, Kevin…can I ask you a question?

Kevin: Sure, Harriet.

Harriet: Well, it's very difficult.

Kevin: Go ahead. Ask me.

Harriet: Well, I read some stories in *The National Questioner* about you, and you're my favorite actor and all, and I just wanted to ask you….

Kevin: Yes?

Harriet: Well, is that really your hair or is it a wig? Oh, I'm sorry. That wasn't very polite.

Kevin: That's OK. It's all mine. You can try it. Give it a good pull…. Argh!

Harriet: Yes, it's yours. I'm very sorry.

Questions

1. What's Harriet eating tonight?
2. What does she usually eat on Mondays?
3. What's her husband doing now?
4. Does she ever drink alcohol?
5. What are they going to drink tonight?
6. What's Kevin doing tonight?

Exercise

She usually eats franks and beans.
tonight/filet mignon
But tonight she's eating filet mignon.

1. She usually eats at home.
   tonight/in a restaurant
2. She usually drinks water.
   tonight/diet soda
3. She often reads about Kevin.
   tonight/talking to him
4. He often has dinner with famous people.
   tonight/Harriet

An accident

Two cars were going down Second Street in Lawrence, Kansas. A middle-aged woman was driving a Chevrolet. Right behind her a teenage student was driving an old Ford. The woman was driving slowly and carefully. The student wasn't driving carefully. He was worrying about his classes in school. He was doing badly in Spanish and physics. He was worrying about the final exams, so he wasn't paying attention to the road. The traffic light was green. A young woman was walking down the street. A cat was sitting on the corner near the traffic light. A dog was sitting on the opposite corner.

The dog was thinking about a bone.

Suddenly the dog saw the cat.

It ran across the road.

The woman saw the dog.

She quickly put her foot on the brakes.

The Ford crashed into the Chevrolet.

A young woman saw the accident.

She ran to a telephone booth.

The police and an ambulance came immediately.

Last night at 9:18 PM, Mr. Scott Shaw, a high school principal, was walking from his office to his car when he was attacked from behind. The attacker hit the principal on the head. The police think the attacker was a student. They are going to question every student in the school—both male and female.

Questions
When did it happen?
What time did it happen?
Where was the principal going?
Where was he coming from?
Did the attacker hit him?
Where did the attacker hit him?
What do the police think?
What are they going to do?

A police officer questioned the victim at the hospital last night:

Police officer: What can you remember about the attack, Mr. Shaw?
Mr. Shaw: Well, I was working late last night.
Police officer: What time did you leave your office?
Mr. Shaw: At about a quarter after nine.
Police officer: Are you sure?
Mr. Shaw: Yes, I am. I looked at my watch.
Police officer: What did you do then?
Mr. Shaw: Well, I locked the office door, and I was walking to the parking lot when somebody hit me on the head.
Police officer: Did you see the attacker?
Mr. Shaw: No. He was wearing a mask over his face.
Police officer: He? Oh, so it was a man!

Mr. Shaw: Well, I'm not really sure. No…no, I don't know.
Police officer: Tell me, Mr. Shaw, how did you break your leg?
Mr. Shaw: Well, when they were putting me into the ambulance, they dropped me!

Questions
Where's the victim now?
What's he doing?
What's the police officer doing?
What was Mr. Shaw doing at 9 PM yesterday?
What time did he leave his office?
Is he sure?
Ask, "Why?"
What did he lock?
When did the attacker hit him?
Did he see the attacker?
Ask, "Why not?"
Was the attacker a man or a woman?
Did Mr. Shaw break his arm?
Ask, "What?"
Ask, "When?"

Pictures from the past

Josh is visiting his mother. He's with his new girlfriend, Rosa.

Rosa: That's a nice picture of Josh, Mrs. Ryan. Did you take it?

Mrs. Ryan: Yes. Photography's my hobby. I have a lot of pictures of Josh.

Rosa: Oh, really? May I see some?

Mrs. R.: Why, yes. There's an album here.

Josh: Oh, no, Mom! Not the photographs! Please!

Rosa: Shh. I want to see them. Oh, wow!

Mrs. R.: Look, Josh could sit up when he was six months old.

Rosa: That's really cute!

Mrs. R.: And he could talk when he was a year…look.

Josh: This is awful. Please, Mom…

Mrs. R.: Be quiet, Joshua. When he was three he could swim.

Rosa: Really? I couldn't swim until I was five or six.

Mrs. R.: This is a picture on the beach…

Josh: Mom! I'm not wearing any clothes in that picture!

6 months   1 year   8 years   10 years

3 years   6 years   14 years   17 years

Exercise 1

Look at the photo album and write sentences about Josh.

Exercise 2

When Josh was ten, he could play the piano, and he could ride a bike. But he couldn't speak French.
Now write ten sentences about yourself:
When I was ten, I could read.
When I was ten, I couldn't speak English.

Exercise 3

Rosa couldn't swim until she was five or six.
Write five sentences about yourself.

Miami Police Squad

Laura: This is a very important job, Duane.

Duane: Right, boss. What do I have to do?

Laura: You have to fly to Bermuda tonight.

Duane: Bermuda, huh? I have a girlfriend there.

Laura: I know that! But you can't visit her.

Duane: Sure, boss. Where do I have to stay?

Laura: You have to go to the Palm Tree Hotel. Stay in your room and wait for Eric. Eric has the Picasso painting.

Duane: Which passport do I have to use?

Laura: The British one. And don't forget, you have to speak with a British accent. They can't discover your real nationality!

Duane: OK. Do I have to drink tea?

Laura: Yes, you do!

Duane: Oh, no, boss! I hate tea.

Questions

Does Duane have to go to Jamaica?
Ask, "Where?" Ask, "When?"
Who can't he visit in Bermuda?
Does he have to stay in a hotel?
Ask, "Which hotel?"
Which passport does he have to use?
Does he have to speak with a French accent?
Ask, "How?" Ask, "Why?"
Does he have to drink tea?
Ask, "Why?"

Tony: OK, Carmen. We have to get that painting. Here's the plan. Go to the Palm Tree Hotel…

Carmen: Do I have to reserve a room?

Tony: No, you don't. We reserved a room for you…next to Duane Skinner's room.

Carmen: Do I have to stay in the room?

Tony: No, you don't, but you have to watch Skinner all the time. You have to find that painting!

Carmen: Do I have to contact you every day?

Tony: No, you can't! It's too dangerous for you.

Carmen: Why?

Tony: Because Duane Skinner's a very dangerous guy.

Carmen: OK. Is that everything?

Tony: Oh, and you have to speak with a British accent. He can't discover that you're an American police officer.

Questions

Where does Carmen have to go?
Does she have to reserve a room?
Ask, "Why not?"
Does she have to stay in the room?
Who does she have to watch?
Can she contact Tony every day?
Ask, "Why not?"
How does she have to speak?
What can't Duane discover?

Exercise

I'm on a diet, so
I can't eat bread.
I can't have
sugar in my
coffee.
I can't go
everywhere by
car.

I'm a millionaire,
so I don't have
to work.
I don't have to
save money.
I don't have to
get up early.

Write six
true sentences.
Begin:
I can't • • • .
I don't have to
• • • .

Telephoning

M: Hello?
N: Hello. Is Akiko Nakamura there?
M: Who's calling, please?
N: Travis Bergman.
M: Please hold.
N: Thanks.
M: Uh, hello. I'm sorry, but Akiko's out.
N: Oh. When do you expect her back?
M: I'm not sure.
N: Could you take a message?
M: Yes, of course.

Please hold.
Just a minute, please.
One moment, please.
Can you hold?

out
not here
not at her desk
in a meeting

O1: Nynex. What city?
P: San Diego.
O1: That's area code 619. Please dial 619-555-1212 for Directory Assistance in that area.

O2: Pacific Bell. What name and city?
P: Gonzalez. 1854 Camelia Drive, San Diego.
Tape: The number is area code 619-451-0239.

Gonzalez, San Diego (619)
Fitzgerald, Birmingham (205)
Costello, Charlotte (704)
Waldheim, Tampa (813)

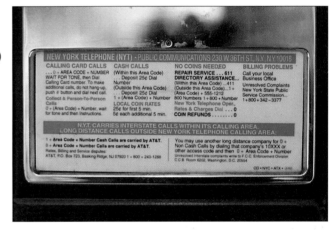

Q: Hotel operator.
R: Hello. Can I call direct to Rio de Janeiro from my room?
Q: Yes. First press 9 for an external line. Wait for a tone, then press the international access number 011.
R: OK. What next?
Q: Then press the country code…55 for Brazil, and the area code.
R: Right. Rio's 21, I think.
Q: That's correct. Then just press the local number.
R: That's great. Thank you.
Q: You're welcome.

Rio de Janiero, Brazil
Kyoto, Japan
Acapulco, Mexico
Maracaibo, Venezuela
Oxford, England

Exercise

Use the telephone instruction card below and make conversations.

SHERLAND TOWERS HOTEL

Press 9 for an external line. Then press 011 for international access. Then press the country code and the area code and number. There are examples below. If you require other codes, call 0 for the hotel operator.

Country	City	Country Code	City Code	Country	City	Country Code	City Code
Australia	Canberra	61	62	Korea, Rep. of	Seoul	82	2
Brazil	Rio de Janeiro	55	21	Mexico	Acapulco	52	748
China	Beijing	86	1	New Zealand	Wellington	64	4
Colombia	Cartagena	57	53	Taiwan	Taipei	886	2
India	Calcutta	91	33	United Kingdom	Oxford	44	865
Indonesia	Jakarta	62	21	Venezuela	Maracaibo	58	61
Japan	Kyoto	81	75				

Names

Ask another student these questions.
- What's your first name?
- Does it have a special meaning?
- Do any of your relatives have the same first name?
- What do your friends call you?
- Is that a nickname?
- What's your last name?
- Does it have a special meaning?
- Do you have a middle name?

CAN MRS. ANASTASIA SAMANTHA ELIZABETH MARY ALEXANDRA FITZGERALD SMYTHE-TURNER PLEASE REPORT TO THE DEPARTURES DESK?

Marital status, family, and home

Ask another student these questions.
- Are you married or single?
- How many brothers and sisters do you have?
- How many aunts and uncles do you have?
- Which people usually give you presents?
- Do you have any children?
- Where were you born?
- Did you go to school there?
- Where do you live now?

SOME JOBS ARE 24 HOURS A DAY, 7 DAYS A WEEK!

Birthdays

Ask another student these questions. Try to guess their birthday!
- On which day of the week were you born?
- Were you born in the summer, fall, winter, or spring?
- Do you know your astrological sign?
- Were you born on an odd-numbered day (1, 3, 5, etc.) or an even-numbered day (2, 4, 6, etc.)?
- Does your birthday have one digit (e.g., 1) or two digits (e.g., 11, 21)?

CONGRATULATIONS, HON!

Education and work

Ask another student these questions.
- Are you still in school full-time?
- What are you studying?
- Do you have any degrees?
- What are they?
- What was your favorite subject in school?
- Do you have a job?
- What do you do for a living? (or What are you going to do?)
- How many hours do you work each week?
- How many days do you work?

Exercise 1

Now complete this form. Then interview another student and find out about their personal history.

Leo	Pisces	Aquarius
Gemini	Aries	Libra	Cancer
Scorpio	Sagittarius	Virgo
Capricorn	Taurus

PERSONAL INFORMATION

DATE OF BIRTH: PLACE OF BIRTH:

MARITAL STATUS:

EDUCATION: ELEMENTARY SCHOOL: _____

     HIGH SCHOOL: _____

     COLLEGE: _____

DEGREES:

WORK RECORD:

On the moon

The *Eagle* has landed on the moon! Astronaut Phil Strongarm is speaking to Mission Control in Houston.

Mission Control: Hello, Phil. Can you hear me?
Strongarm: Yes, I can hear you clearly.
Mission Control: What are you going to do next?
Strongarm: I'm going to open the door.

Mission Control: Hello, Phil. What are you doing now?
Strongarm: I'm opening the door.

Mission Control: Phil! Have you opened the door?
Strongarm: Yes, I've opened it! I can see the moon, and it's fantastic!

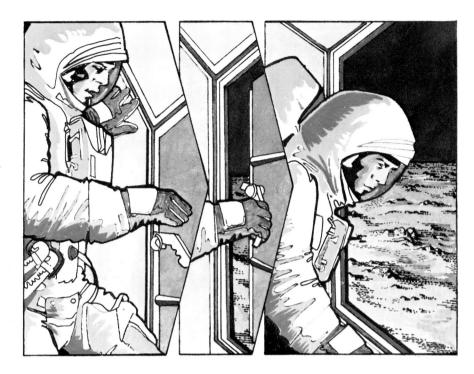

Exercise

1. What's he going to do?
   He's going to climb down the ladder.

What's he doing?
He's climb**ing** down the ladder.

What has he done?
He's climb**ed** down the ladder.

2. What's he going to do?
   He's going to raise the flag.

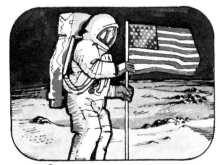

• • • • ?
• • • • .

• • • • ?
• • • • .

3. What's he going to do?
   He's going to close the door.

• • • • ?
• • • • .

• • • • ?
• • • • .

Kelly: OK. Which way is the car?

Mark: It's in space 34. It's this way.

Kelly: I can't see it.

Mark: No, Kelly. It's gone!

Kelly: Are you sure?

Mark: Yes. It was in space 34. It isn't there now. It's gone, Kelly. It really has gone. This is terrible! It's only two months old.

Kelly: Come on! Where's it gone? This is a high-security parking garage. You can't get out without the ticket, and you have the ticket.

Mark: But space 34 is empty—and it's the right number. I wrote it on the ticket.

Kelly: Let me see. Oh, Mark. It hasn't gone! We're on the wrong floor! Look, this is floor C. The car's on floor D.

Paul: Hey, Bill, can you lend me $10?

Bill: Sorry, I can't. I haven't been to the bank today.

Paul: Oh, I haven't been there either, and I need some money. We could go now.

Bill: No, the bank's closed. It's too late. Why don't you ask Pete?

Paul: Has he been to the bank?

Bill: Yes, he has. He always goes to the bank on Mondays.

Exercise

She's *been to the* bank.

He . . . supermarket.

They . . . library.

He . . . hairdresser.

She's *gone to* Paris.

They . . . Boston.

He . . . the hospital.

She . . . Los Angeles on business.

What have you done?

S: Oh, no!
T: What's wrong?
S: I can't find my pen.
T: Really? Ha ha ha.
S: It isn't funny.
T: Oh, yes it is.
S: It is? I don't understand.
T: Well, you have to look carefully.
S: I've looked everywhere.
T: No, you haven't. Look behind your ear.
S: Oh.

pen
pencil
address book
checkbook

behind your ear
in your hand
in your pocket
on your desk
under your elbow

U: Watch out! I've just washed the floor.
V: No, you haven't.
U: Yes, I have.
V: Well, you haven't done a very good job. Look over there. You've missed a spot.
U: You're right. Here's the mop.

floor
walls
windows
mirrors

mop
sponge
rag
bucket

X: I'm so bored.
Y: Well, do something.
X: What, for example?
Y: Wash your hair.
X: I've already washed it.
Y: Call your friend Susan.
X: I've already talked to her today.
Y: Clean your room.
X: I've already cleaned it.
Y: Then do the dishes.
X: Haven't you done them yet?
Y: No, I haven't.
X: Oh, all right.

wash/hair
finish/homework
iron/clothes
brush/teeth
do/homework

Questionnaire

Which of these things have you done today? Complete the questionnaire.

QUESTIONNAIRE				
● Have you brushed your	**teeth** today?	Yes ☐	No ☐	
	hair	Yes ☐	No ☐	
	shoes	Yes ☐	No ☐	
● Have you telephoned	**a friend** today?	Yes ☐	No ☐	
	a coworker	Yes ☐	No ☐	
	a relative	Yes ☐	No ☐	
● Have you watched TV today?		Yes ☐	No ☐	
● Have you listened to music today?		Yes ☐	No ☐	

Exercise 1

Interview another student. How did they answer the questions?

Exercise 2

Write sentences about another student.
He has ● ● ● today.
She hasn't ● ● ● today.

Gina: Jeff! I've got a new job! I'm going to live in New York.

Jeff: You are? I lived in New York five years ago.

Gina: Did you like it?

Jeff: Not very much.

Gina: Why not?

Jeff: Well, there were too many people, and there was too much noise.

Gina: I love crowds and noise!

Jeff: Well, I don't. And I don't like pollution.

Gina: What do you mean?

Jeff: There isn't enough fresh air in New York.

Gina: But you can go to concerts and the ballet and Broadway and…

Jeff: I never had enough money for all that. The rents are very high.

Gina: Why is that?

Jeff: Because there aren't enough apartments.

Gina: Well, I still prefer big cities.

Jeff: But why?

Gina: I was born in a small town. It was too quiet and too dull.

Jeff: You were lucky.

Gina: I don't think so. There wasn't much to do. That's why young people go to New York.

Jeff: But New York's too expensive for young people.

Gina: They still go. They want excitement.

Jeff: Well, I don't want excitement. I just want a quiet life, that's all.

Exercise

In New York
There's too much noise.
There isn't enough fresh air.
There are too many people.
There aren't enough apartments.

In the world
1. . . . pollution.
2. . . . oil.
3. . . . people.
4. . . . doctors.

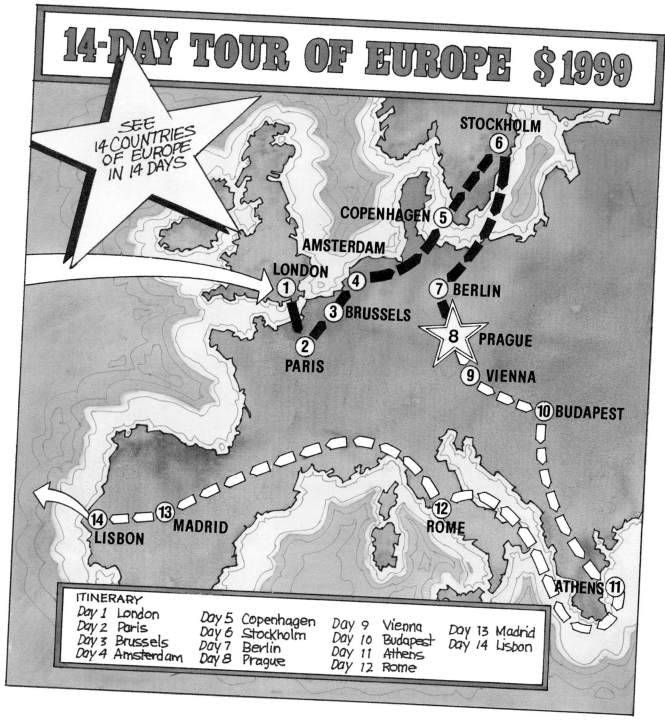

14-DAY TOUR OF EUROPE $1999

SEE 14 COUNTRIES OF EUROPE IN 14 DAYS

STOCKHOLM ⑥
COPENHAGEN ⑤
AMSTERDAM
LONDON ① ④ ⑦ BERLIN
③ BRUSSELS
② ⑧ PRAGUE
PARIS ⑨ VIENNA
⑩ BUDAPEST
⑭ ⑬ MADRID ⑫ ROME
LISBON ATHENS ⑪

ITINERARY
Day 1 London
Day 2 Paris
Day 3 Brussels
Day 4 Amsterdam
Day 5 Copenhagen
Day 6 Stockholm
Day 7 Berlin
Day 8 Prague
Day 9 Vienna
Day 10 Budapest
Day 11 Athens
Day 12 Rome
Day 13 Madrid
Day 14 Lisbon

Elmer Colt is from Kansas. He's on a 14-day tour of Europe. The tour started in London. At the moment he's in Prague. It's the eighth day of the tour. He's already been to seven countries and stayed in the principal cities.

He's never been to Europe before, and he's already seen a lot of new places. He's done a lot of interesting things, and the tour hasn't finished yet.

Exercise 1

Elmer's been to London, but he hasn't been to Vienna yet.
Write four sentences about Elmer.

Exercise 2

I've been to Paris, but I haven't been to London yet.
Write four sentences about yourself.

Exercise 3

Answer these questions with *Yes, I have* or *No, I haven't*.
1. Have you been to California?
2. Have you been to New York?
3. Have you been to Europe?
4. Have you been to Australia?
5. Have you been to a rock concert?
6. Have you been to an American movie?

Elmer calls home

Elmer: Hello, Mom? Is that you?

Mrs. Colt: Oh, Elmer, yes. How are you? Where are you now?

Elmer: I'm fine. I've just arrived in Prague, Mom.

Mrs. Colt: You haven't sent us any postcards yet.

Elmer: Yes, I have. I've sent one from every city.

Mrs. Colt: Have you been to Paris yet, Elmer?

Elmer: Yes, I have.

Mrs. Colt: Have you been to Vienna yet?

Elmer: No, I haven't. We're going to Vienna tomorrow.

Mrs. Colt: Elmer! Are you still there?

Elmer: Yes, Mom.

Mrs. Colt: How many countries have you seen now?

Elmer: Well, this is the eighth day, so I've already seen eight countries.

Mrs. Colt: Have you spent much money?

Elmer: Well, uh, yes, Mom. I've bought a lot of souvenirs, and I want to buy some more. Can you send me a thousand dollars?

Mrs. Colt: All right, Elmer.

Mrs. Colt: Elmer, are you listening to me?

Elmer: Sure, Mom.

Mrs. Colt: Have you taken many pictures, Elmer?

Elmer: Yes, I've taken a lot. I've used three rolls of film!

Mrs. Colt: Have you met any nice girls yet?

Elmer: Oh, yes, Mom. There's a girl from Texas on the tour. We've done everything together.

Mrs. Colt: Elmer! Elmer! Are you still there?

Exercise 1

postcards

How many postcards *has he sent?*
He's sent one from every city.

Write questions and answers with:
1. cities
2. money
3. souvenirs
4. photographs
5. rolls of film

Exercise 2

Have you ever bought a souvenir?
Yes, I have.
No, I haven't.

Answer these questions:
Have you ever seen the Golden Gate Bridge?
Have you ever been to Paris?
Have you ever sent a postcard?
Have you ever spent a lot of money on a trip?
Have you ever met a Texan?
Have you ever taken pictures on a trip?

A: Have you ever studied a language before?
B: Yes, I have.
A: Oh, which one did you study?
B: I studied Spanish in high school.

in high school
in college
in night school
at home
overseas

C: Have you ever been to a big wedding?
D: Yes, I have.
C: Whose wedding was it?
D: It was my brother's.

brother's
sister's
cousin's
friend's
neighbor's

E: Have you ever seen a fire?
F: Uh, yes, I have.
E: When did you see it?
F: I saw a bad fire in Detroit in 1992.

in 1992
in 1989
in 1993
in 1990
in 1987

G: Have you ever eaten sushi?
H: Yes, I have.
G: Where did you eat it?
H: Maria and I ate sushi in Hawaii last year.

sushi/Hawaii
snails/Paris
steak tartare/The Grand Hotel
alligator tail/Florida
buffalo steak/San Francisco

I: Have you ever had the flu?
J: Yes, I have.
I: When did you have it?
J: I had it last winter.

last winter
last spring
last summer
last fall
last year

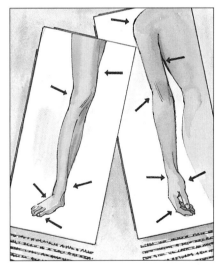

K: Have you ever broken a bone?
L: Yes, I have.
K: What did you break?
L: I broke my leg.

leg/toe/foot/ankle/knee
finger/hand/wrist/arm/elbow/
shoulder

Dr. Finkel is an inventor. He has just designed a new machine. The machine can change people. His assistant, Boris, is going to try the machine for the first time.

Boris: Is it safe, doctor?
Finkel: Oh, yes. Yes, of course it is, Boris.
Boris: I'm afraid, doctor.
Finkel: Nonsense! This machine is going to change you! You're going to be a better person, Boris. Stronger! Uh, thinner! Healthier! Happier!
Boris: I'm happy now, doctor.
Finkel: Well, you're going to be happier. And more intelligent.
Boris: I'm intelligent now, doctor.
Finkel: Uh, yes. Well, you're less intelligent than I am, Boris. Just get into the machine…
Boris: But doctor…ooh! Uh! … Wah! Wah!
Finkel: Hmm. Yes. And younger, too. Sorry about that, Boris.
Boris: Mommy! I want my mommy….

Exercise 1

Canada's cold but Greenland's *colder*.
Make sentences with these words:
hot/wet/high

Exercise 3

Patsy's better than Mike in math.
Mike's worse than Patsy in math.
Make sentences with these words:
English/History/Geography/French/Science

Exercise 2

Nathan's older than Kevin.
Kevin's younger than Nathan.
Make sentences with these words:
1. tall/short
2. small/big
3. light/heavy

Nathan   Kevin

Exercise 4

A car's more expensive than a motorcycle.
A motorcycle's less comfortable than a car.
Make sentences with these words:
dangerous/economical/convenient

Jerry Floyd is talking to his grandfather about his new job:

"It's terrible, Grandpa. I have to get up at seven o'clock because I have to catch the bus to work. Because I'm new, I have to make the coffee at work. I have to work hard during the week. I'm only happy on weekends. I don't have to work then."

Questions
Does Jerry have to get up at six o'clock?
Does he have to get up at seven o'clock?
Does he have to catch the train?
Does he have to catch the bus?
Does he have to make the tea?
Does he have to make the coffee?
Does he have to work hard during the week?
Does he have to work hard on weekends?

His grandfather isn't very sympathetic:

"I had to start work when I was fourteen. I lived in West Virginia, and there wasn't much work. I had to work in the coal mines. We had to work twelve hours a day. We didn't have to work on Sundays, but we had to work the other six days of the week."

Questions
Did he have to start work when he was 15, or did he have to start work when he was 14?
Did he live in Pennsylvania, or did he live in West Virginia?
Did he have to work in a factory or in a coal mine?
Did he have to work 8 hours a day, or did he have to work 12 hours a day?
Did he have to work on Sundays?
Did he have to work five days a week, or did he have to work six days a week?

"When I was eighteen, World War II started. I joined the army. I had to wear a uniform, and I had to go to Europe. We had to obey the officers. A lot of my friends died."

Questions
When did World War II start?
What did he join?
What did he have to wear?
Where did he have to go?
Who did he have to obey?
How many of his friends died?

"When I was sixty, I had to go into the hospital because of the dust from the mines. It was the only quiet time in my life. I didn't have to work, and I didn't have to earn money."

Questions
Did he have to go to the hospital?
When did he have to go to the hospital?
Why did he have to go to the hospital?
Did he have to work in the hospital?
Did he have to earn money?

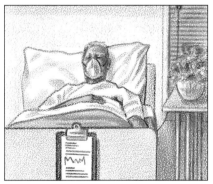

"I retired when I was sixty-five. Nowadays I don't work, and I don't have to get up early. But I have to live on my pension, and life is still difficult. So, Jerry, I don't feel sorry for you."

Questions
Did he retire at 60?
Ask, "When?"
What doesn't he have to do now?
Does he earn money now?
What does he live on?
Is life easy for him now, or is it difficult?
Does he feel sorry for his grandson?

The trivia game

Candice: OK. It's my turn. Three. One, two, three. I'm on blue.

Jeremy: Blue. That's Geography. What's the biggest country in the world?

Candice: Uh, Canada.

Jeremy: No. Russia's bigger than Canada. It's the biggest country in the world.

Candice: That's not right! In my geography book, the U.S.S.R. **was** the biggest, but Russia is smaller than the U.S.S.R.

Jeremy: It doesn't matter, Candice. Russia **is** smaller than the U.S.S.R., but it's still bigger than Canada. Your turn, Megan.

Megan: OK. Six! What's that?

Jeremy: Nature. What is the most intelligent animal in the world?

Megan: That's easy. Humans are the most intelligent.

Jeremy: No.

Megan: What do you mean, "no"?

Jeremy: The answer on the card is whales. Whales have the biggest brains.

Megan: But that's not the same thing!

Jeremy: That's the answer on the card. OK, it's my turn.

Exercise 1

Make conversations with these cards:

GEOGRAPHY

Q. Which is the highest mountain in the world?

GEOGRAPHY

A. Mount Everest (8,848 meters or 29,028 feet).

NATURE

Q. Which is the largest animal in the world?

NATURE

A. The Blue Whale. (Up to 33 meters long. Weight 190 tons).

TRANSPORTATION

Q.. What is the world's most expensive car?

TRANSPORTATION

A. The American President's 1969 Lincoln Continental Executive. (It cost $500,000 at 1969 prices!)

<table>
<tr><th colspan="4">High School Grades</th></tr>
<tr><td></td><td>Alan</td><td>Robert</td><td>Tony</td></tr>
<tr><td>English</td><td>A</td><td>B+</td><td>B</td></tr>
<tr><td>Math</td><td>C</td><td>D</td><td>A</td></tr>
<tr><td>History</td><td>B</td><td>A</td><td>C</td></tr>
<tr><td>Spanish</td><td>A-</td><td>A</td><td>A+</td></tr>
<tr><td>Music</td><td>A</td><td>C-</td><td>B</td></tr>
</table>

Exercise 2

Tricia's the tallest.
Amber's the oldest.
Make sentences with these words:
1. light/heavy **2.** old/young
3. small/big

Exercise 3

Alan's the best in English.
Robert's the worst in math.
Make sentences about:
English/Math/History/Spanish/Music

Exercise 4

The Cadillac's the most expensive.
The Grand Am's the least expensive.
Make sentences with these words:
modern/beautiful/comfortable

CN Tower

Jodie and Adam are on vacation in Toronto. They're visiting the CN Tower.

Jodie: Did you get the tickets?
Adam: Yes. They're here. Where's the line for the elevators?
Jodie: It's this way. Are you OK, Adam?
Adam: Uh…yes. It's just…well…I don't like heights, that's all.

Adam: Uh, I feel dizzy.
Jodie: The view's better over here, Adam. You can see farther.
Adam: Don't go too near the window.
Jodie: Come on! You can see the city better from here.
Adam: What's that down there?
Jodie: It's an airplane. It's landing at the airport.
Adam: But it's below us.

Jodie: Can we go up to the space deck? That's the highest level. It's 33 stories higher than this one.
Adam: What? Do we have to?
Jodie: It's the highest public observation gallery in the world. We have to see it.
Adam: Uh…all right.

Jodie: This is fantastic! It's the most exciting place I've ever been to! Think about it, Adam…we're on the tallest building in the world!
Adam: I *am* thinking about it.
Jodie: Come over here. This is the best view. You can see Niagara Falls…and it's 100 miles away. Oh, sorry. Are you OK?
Adam: Not really. I feel worse!

Adam: Ah! We're on the ground again. I feel better already.
Jodie: Thanks for coming up with me.
Adam: That's OK, Jodie. Do you know something? I'm not going to be afraid of heights again!

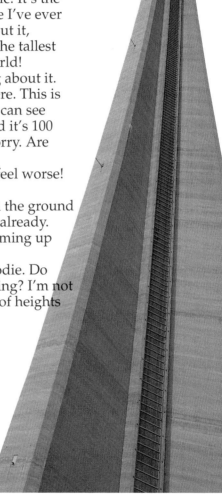

Facts

The CN Tower is the tallest free-standing structure in the world. It is 1,815 feet tall (553.33 meters).
The Sky Pod is 1,140 feet (347.5 meters) above the ground. It has two observation decks; one is indoors, the other is outdoors. It is seven stories high.
From the Sky Pod, you can travel 33 stories higher to the Space Deck. This is 1,465 feet (447 meters) high and it is the highest observation gallery in the world.
You can watch planes at the Toronto Island airport—right below you.

Exercise

a. CN Tower/tall
b. CN Tower/Eiffel Tower, Paris
c. CN Tower/the world

a. Concorde airplane/fast
b. It/a Boeing 747
c. It/the world

a. Mount Everest/high
b. It/Mount McKinley
c. It/the world

a. Rolls-Royce car/comfortable
b. It/Corvette
c. It/the world

a. The view/good
b. It/from the Eiffel Tower
c. It/the world

Write sentences like this:
a. *The CN Tower's very tall.*
b. *It's taller than the Eiffel Tower in Paris.*
c. *It's the tallest tower in the world.*

Mr. Burnette: Come in!

Withers: Sir?

Mr. Burnette: Who are you?

Withers: My name's Withers, sir. I'm your new personal assistant.

Mr. Burnette: Where's Mrs. Sherman? I want my coffee!

Withers: I'll get it, sir.

Withers: There you go, sir.

Mr. Burnette: Thank you, Smithers.

Withers: Uh…it's "Withers," sir.

Mr. Burnette: It's hot in here. Will you open the window, please?

Withers: Yes, sir. I'll get you a glass of iced water, too.

Mr. Burnette: Good. Please be quick.

Mr. Burnette: Will you bring me the "suggestions" box, Zithers.

Withers: Of course I will, sir. Uh…where is it?

Mr. Burnette: In the cafeteria. People can put suggestions about the company in it.

Withers: I'll get it right away.

Mr. Burnette: All right, Blithers. Let's see it!

Withers: There are a lot of suggestions, sir.

Mr. Burnette: Well, let's hear them!

Withers: Yes, sir. This is the first one. "Why doesn't Burnette speak politely to people?" Next, "Why don't the bosses remember our names?" And another, "Why don't we begin work at 11 AM? Old Burnette does." And another…

Mr. Burnette: "Old Burnette," eh? Who wrote the suggestions? Did they sign them?

Withers: Uh, no, sir.

Mr. Burnette: Find their names, Zithers.

Withers: I will, sir.

Mr. Burnette: And don't tell anybody about the suggestions.

Withers: I won't, sir.

Exercise

Complete the spaces with words from the box.

will/Let's/won't/I'll/Why don't

Requests

A: • • • you close the door, please?
B: Yes, I • • • •

A: • • • you lend me $100?
B: No, I • • • •

Offers

A: I'm thirsty.
B: • • • get you a glass of water.

A: It's very cold in here.
B: • • • close the window.

Suggestions

A: There's no food in the fridge.
B: • • • we go to a restaurant?

A: There's a good movie at the AMC.
B: • • • go and see it.

Comparing things

A: Are you ready?
B: Yes. Let's go down for breakfast.
A: I like your room.
B: It's the same as yours.
A: No, it isn't. It's different from mine.
B: Is it?
A: Yes, it is. It's bigger, and it has a better view.

down for breakfast
down for dinner
find a cab
to the coffee shop

bigger/better view
smaller/less comfortable
nicer/more interesting

C: Hi, Sarah. Good to see you.
A: Good to see you, Sam. Are you staying here?
C: No. I'm at the Ambassador. It's down the street.
A: How is it?
C: Well, it isn't as modern as this hotel, but it's very comfortable.
A: How long have you been at this conference?
C: As long as you have. Two days.
A: That's funny. I haven't seen you before.
C: Really? I saw you in the coffee shop. I waved, but you didn't see me.

not as modern/ comfortable
not as good/cheap
not as clean/ convenient
not as large/ interesting

A: Did you enjoy that presentation?
B: Not really. Did you?
A: No. I've heard a lot of boring speakers before, but he's the most boring speaker I've ever heard!
B: Are you going to the next presentation?
A: No. Are you?
B: No, I'm not. Let's go and have a cup of coffee.

hear/boring speakers
listen to/interesting speakers
see/good videos
hear/bad speeches

have a cup of coffee
take a walk
have some lunch
look in the gift shop

Exercise

Compare these hotel rooms.

A: Good morning.
B: Good morning. How can I help you?
A: I want some seats for Tuesday night. Are there any left?
B: No, I'm very sorry. There are no seats left. Every seat is reserved.

C: Doctor, I think there's something in my eye.
D: Let me have a look.
C: Everything looks funny and it hurts.
D: I can't see anything. No, I'm sure there's nothing there.

E: There's somebody in the other office!
F: I didn't hear anybody.
E: Take a look, please.
F: OK. No, there's nobody there. Everybody's gone home.

G: What are you looking for?
H: My pen. It's somewhere in this room.
G: Have you looked everywhere?
H: Yes, but I can't find it anywhere.

Study this:

	PLACE	PERSON	THING
Some	somewhere	someone somebody	something
any?	anywhere?	anyone? anybody?	anything?
no	nowhere	no one nobody	nothing
not...any	not anywhere	not anyone not anybody	not anything
every	everywhere	everyone everybody	everything

Exercise

Complete the spaces with words from the boxes.

> something/someone/anything/anyone

There's *something* in my soup.
There's . . . in the other room.
Is there . . . in the refrigerator?
Is there . . . in the bathroom?
There isn't . . . in the cabinet.

> anywhere/everywhere/
> nothing/something

I can't find it. I've looked . . . .
There's . . . to eat for dinner.
Would you like . . . to drink?
I want to stay home. I don't want to go . . . .

Four lives

Herbert Burke, James Brody, Gina Rossi, and Charles Phillips all went to the same school. They finished elementary school in 1978 and high school in 1984. They've had very different careers.

Herbie Burke became a politician four years ago. He's very successful. He bought a country house three years ago and bought a Jaguar at the same time. He's been a Congressman for four years.

Questions

When did Herbie Burke become a politician?
When did he buy a country house?
When did he buy a Jaguar?
How long has he been a Congressman?
How long has he had his house?
How long has he had his car?

Exercise

He's been there *since* 1993.
They've been there *for* five years.

Complete these sentences
1. She's had that watch . . . three weeks.
2. We've been here . . . January.

Jimmy Brody was very lucky. He won a lottery in 1991 and moved to a Pacific island. He bought a luxury yacht the next year. He's still on the island. He's been there since 1991. He's had his yacht since 1992.

Questions

When did Jimmy win the lottery?
Where did he move to?
What did he buy?
When did he buy it?
Where is he now?
How long has he been there?
How long has he had his yacht?

3. I've had my camera . . . two years.
4. They've been married . . . 1990.
5. He's had his car . . . two months.
6. Jorge's been in the United States . . . March.

Gina Rossi and Charlie Phillips fell in love at school. He gave her a ring when they finished high school. She wears it every day, and she's never taken it off. They got married in 1988, and they're still in love. They moved to Arizona in 1993.

Questions

When did Gina and Charlie fall in love?
When did he give her the ring?
Has she ever taken it off?
When did they get married?
Are they still in love?
When did they move to Arizona?
How long has she had the ring?
How long have they been married?
How long have they been in Arizona?

An electronic world?

Flight attendant: Pardon me, sir. Is everything here yours?

Mr. Gabriel: Yes, that's right.

Attendant: I'm sorry, sir. You can't use any electronic equipment during takeoff and landing.

Mr. Gabriel: Why not?

Attendant: It's an airline regulation, sir. You can use the CD player during the flight, but I'm afraid you can't use the laptop computer or the portable phone…or the portable TV.

Mr. Gabriel: But I have to use my computer. I need it!

Attendant: I'm very sorry.

Mr. Gabriel: But I can't live without it! What am I going to do for two hours?

Attendant: You can read, sir.

Mr. Gabriel: Read? But I don't have any books.

Attendant: I'll get you a magazine, sir.

Questions

Can he use any electronic equipment during takeoff?

Can he use it during landing?

Which things can't he use during the flight?

What's he going to do during the flight?

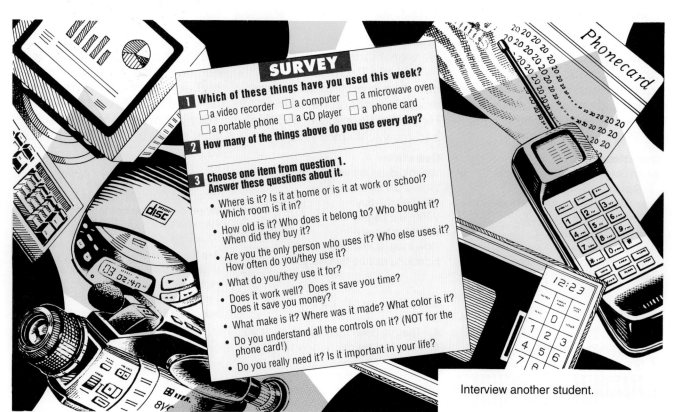

SURVEY

1 Which of these things have you used this week?

☐ a video recorder ☐ a computer ☐ a microwave oven
☐ a portable phone ☐ a CD player ☐ a phone card

2 How many of the things above do you use every day?

3 Choose one item from question 1. Answer these questions about it.

- Where is it? Is it at home or is it at work or school? Which room is it in?
- How old is it? Who does it belong to? Who bought it? When did they buy it?
- Are you the only person who uses it? Who else uses it? How often do you/they use it?
- What do you/they use it for?
- Does it work well? Does it save you time? Does it save you money?
- What make is it? Where was it made? What color is it?
- Do you understand all the controls on it? (NOT for the phone card!)
- Do you really need it? Is it important in your life?

Interview another student.

Battle of the Bands

This is the national *Battle of the Bands* contest. All of the bands have played, and in a moment we're going to hear the result of the contest. The two finalists are Dixie Chickens and Technocrat. All of the members of Technocrat are from Philadelphia. They're on the left—all of them are wearing black suits and silver shirts. All of the members of Dixie Chickens are from Atlanta, Georgia. None of them are wearing suits.

The announcer is Tina Rivera. She's standing with one of the members of Dixie Chickens and one of the members of Technocrat. Both of them are guitarists. Neither of them has been on TV before. Both of them are nervous and neither of them is smiling!

Now the judges have voted, and Tina has announced the result. Dixie Chickens have won the contest! All of them are smiling. The members of Technocrat aren't happy. None of them are smiling. Some of the people in the audience are cheering, but some of them are booing.

Some of them preferred Dixie Chickens but some of them preferred Technocrat. The prizes are great—both of the bands are going to get record contracts.

Exercise

One of them is a guitarist.	. . . drummer.
Both of them are guitarists.	. . . drummers.
Neither of them is a guitarist.	. . . drummer.
Some of them are happy.	. . . wearing suits.
All of them are happy.	. . . wearing suits.
None of them are happy.	. . . wearing suits.

THE WEEKLY GAZETTE

Thursday, May 20   **Marion, North Carolina**   **75¢**

SENSATIONAL JEWEL ROBBERY

Elm Street–Quiet after the robbery

$50,000 STOLEN

THERE WAS A $50,000 JEWEL robbery on Elm Street last Tuesday. The thieves threw a rock through the window of Williston & Company and stole necklaces, rings, and watches worth $50,000. Mr. William Williston, the owner of the store, was working in his office when it happened. The police are looking for three suspects. The thieves drove away in a stolen Lexus Coupé. The police have not found the getaway car yet.

Mr. Williston will give a reward of $2,000 to anyone with information about the thieves. Get in touch with the local police station.

EVEREST EXPEDITION FAILS

AN INTERNATIONAL TEAM OF climbers in the Himalayas wanted to reach the top of Mount Everest yesterday, but they failed because the weather was too bad. They had to postpone the climb until next week. The weather has been the worst since 1989. The three climbers are from Mexico, Japan, and the United States.

ANIMAL ATTACKS

FARMER AARON CROCKETT OF McDowell County is worried about a series of attacks on animals. Something has attacked and killed seven cows on his dairy farm during the last month. There are some bears and wildcats up in the Blue Ridge Mountains, but no one has seen a bear near Crockett's farm for 20 years. McDowell County police say, "Maybe it's a large dog. Nobody saw the attacks." Mr. Crockett is

guarding his fields at night with a shotgun.

RUNAWAY TEENAGER

JANIS ROBERTS, 15 YEARS OLD, OF 1647 Sunrise Road, Marion, left her home last week. She was on her way to school, and nobody has seen her since, Janis's friend, Polly Reyes, told police yesterday.

Janis was wearing blue jeans, a green T-shirt, a white raincoat, and tan boots. She has short blond hair and blue eyes. Please call 461-4600 with any information.

A: Can I help you?
B: Yes, I want to send some flowers to my mother in Chicago.
A: What kind of flowers would you like?
B: Well, what do you recommend?
A: Roses are very nice at this time of year.
B: OK. A dozen pink roses, please.
A: Would you like to include a message?
B: Yes. Just say, "Happy Birthday, Mom. Love, Cindy."

roses

tulips

carnations

daffodils

a dozen (12)
half a dozen (6)
two dozen (24)
ten (10)

C: Mrs. Martinez?
D: Yes, Paul?
C: This is a present for you.
D: A present for me? What a nice surprise. Can I open it now?
C: Yes, of course.
D: Ooh! Candy! I love candy. Thank you very, very much, Paul.
C: Thank *you*, Mrs. Martinez. You've been very kind to me.

a present
a gift
something

candy
cookies
perfume
fruit

E: It's been a wonderful party. Thank you very much.
F: But you can't go yet! The party's just beginning!
E: I'm sorry, but I really have to. I have to catch the last train.
F: Don't be silly. I'll give you a ride. Where are you going?
E: Montreal!
F: Oh, well. Thanks for coming, and thanks for the present.
E: You're very welcome. I'll see you soon.
F: See you.

catch the last train
get up early tomorrow
be home by 11:30
get a ride in Jack's car

Montreal
Caracas
Tokyo
Istanbul
Rio

Exercise
Thanking someone and leaving

You have been to dinner with a friend.
Make a conversation.

> **A** Say good night and thank your friend for dinner.

> **B** Say you enjoyed the dinner, too. Ask **A** not to leave yet.

> **A** Say you have to go.

> **B** Ask, "Why?"

> **A** Think of a good reason! (Begin: Because…)

> **B** Offer something (a ride home? use of the telephone? coffee?)

> **A** Say thank you—but refuse the offer. Say good night.

> **B** Thank **A** for coming.

What have you learned from *New American Streamline Departures*?

Put the verbs in parentheses ( ) in the correct tenses, then act out the conversation.

A: Where . . . (are) you yesterday? I phoned last night but you . . . (aren't) home.

B: I . . . (go) to the movies.

A: Oh, really? What . . . (do) you see?

B: I . . . (see) *The Last Buffalo.* Have you . . . (see) it?

A: No, I haven't. . . . (Is) it good?

B: Yes, it was. It's the best movie I've . . . (see) this year.

Complete the spaces with words from the box, then act out the conversation.

no one	anybody	somebody
	anything	

C: There's . . . at the door!

D: Can't you answer it?

C: No, I can't. I'm in the shower. I'm not wearing . . . !

D: OK, I'll answer it.

(later)

C: Who was it?

D: . . . .

C: What do you mean? I heard the doorbell.

D: Well, I opened the door, but there wasn't . . . there.

Complete the spaces, then act out the conversation.

E: . . . I borrow $20? The check from my parents hasn't . . . yet.

F: I'm very . . . . I can't lend you . . . money. I'm broke.

E: What can I do? I need . . . money. I . . . to go to the supermarket.

F: Why . . . you ask Tammy? She . . . has some money.

E: OK. Thanks.

This is a postcard from a store in Florida. Use it, and choose the best message for you.

Place Stamp Here

TO:
_____
_____
_____

Instant Postcard

INSTANT POSTCARD - 35 cents
It's EASY! Circle the best sentences for you, address the postcard on the other side, buy a stamp, and send it home!

Dear......

● I've missed   you   a lot   this week.
               home   very much
               the family pretty much
               my dog   a little

● This hotel is the   best   I have ever stayed in.
                      worst
                      biggest
                      ugliest

● The hotel food is   not as good as   the food at home. I   like   it here.
                      worse than   don't like
                      better than   love
                      more expensive than   hate

● Yesterday, I went to a theme park   and   went on some rides.
                        a shopping mall   bought souvenirs.
                        a swimming pool   went swimming.
                        a library   read a book.

● All   of the people here are very   friendly.
  None   nice.
  Some   rich.
  A few   suntanned.

● I'll write to you next week.
                     tomorrow.
                     soon.
                     one day.

Lots of love,   - - - - - - - - - - - - - - - -
Love,
Best wishes,
Regards,

Write a postcard like this one, but use **your** ideas.

Vocabulary

This index contains all the words in the Student Book,
and the number of the page where they first occur.

Irregular verbs

Infinitive form	Past tense	Past participle	Infinitive form	Past tense	Past participle
be	was/were	been	let	let	let
become	became	become	lose	lost	lost
begin	began	begun	make	made	made
break	broke	broken	mean	meant	meant
bring	brought	brought	meet	met	met
build	built	built	pay	paid	paid
buy	bought	bought	put	put	put
catch	caught	caught	read	read	read
choose	chose	chosen	ride	rode	ridden
come	came	come	ring	rang	rung
cost	cost	cost	run	ran	run
cut	cut	cut	say	said	said
do	did	done	see	saw	seen
drink	drank	drunk	sell	sold	sold
drive	drove	driven	send	sent	sent
eat	ate	eaten	shine	shone	shone
fall	fell	fallen	show	showed	shown
feel	felt	felt	shut	shut	shut
fight	fought	fought	sing	sang	sung
find	found	found	sit	sat	sat
fly	flew	flown	sleep	slept	slept
forget	forgot	forgotten	speak	spoke	spoken
freeze	froze	frozen	spend	spent	spent
get	got	gotten	stand	stood	stood
give	gave	given	steal	stole	stolen
go	went	gone	swim	swam	swum
grow	grew	grown	take	took	taken
have	had	had	teach	taught	taught
hear	heard	heard	tear	tore	torn
hide	hid	hidden	tell	told	told
hit	hit	hit	think	thought	thought
hurt	hurt	hurt	throw	threw	thrown
keep	kept	kept	wake	woke	woken
know	knew	known	wear	wore	worn
leave	left	left	win	won	won
lend	lent	lent	write	wrote	written

Grammar summaries

Unit 1

To Be: Singular

I	'm / am	a student. / from the United States.
You	're / are	
He / She	's / is	

Am	I	a student?
Are	you	from the United States?
Is	he / she	

Yes,	I am.
	you are.
	he is.
	she is.

No,	I	'm not. / am not.
	you / you	aren't. / are not.
	he / she	isn't / is not.

Unit 2

To Be: Plural

We / You / They	're / are / aren't / are not	American. / Japanese. / Spanish.

Are	we / you / they	American?

Yes,	we / you / they	are.

No,	we / you / they	aren't. / are not.

Unit 3

Demonstratives

What	's / is	that?
	is	it?

This	is	a pen.
That	's / is	an egg.
It	is	

(Unit 3 continued)

Is	this / that / it	a pen? / an egg?

Yes, it is.
No, it isn't.

What are	these? / those? / they?

These / Those / They	are / aren't	pens. / eggs.

Are	these / those / they	pens? / eggs?

Yes, they are.
No, they aren't.

Unit 4

Possessive adjectives

What's	my / your / his / her	job?

I'm	a secretary.
You're	a teacher.
He's	a pilot.
She's	a mechanic.

What are	our / your / their	jobs?

We're	waiters.
You're	teachers.
They're	flight attendants.

Is this your book / Are these your books	here?

Is that your book / Are those your books	over there?

Unit 5

To Be + Adjectives

I	'm	cold.
	am	hot.
He	's	old.
She	is	tired.
It		hungry.
You	're	thirsty.
We	are	
They		

I	'm not	cold.
	am not	hot.
He	isn't	old.
She	is not	tired.
It		hungry.
You	aren't	thirsty.
We	are not	
They		

Am	I	young?
		beautiful?
Is	he	strong?
	she	
	it	
Are	you	
	we	
	they	

Yes	I	am.
	it	
	she	is.
	he	
No,	I	'm not.
		am not.
	it	
	she	's not.
	he	isn't.

Unit 6

There is/There are
a/some/any/no

There	's	a stove.
	isn't	an apple.
	is not	
	are	some cups.
	aren't	any glasses.
	are not	

Is there a stove/an apple?

Yes, there is/No, there isn't.

Are there any cups?

Yes, there are/No, there aren't.

(Unit 6 continued)

| Where | is it? |
| | are they? |

It's	in	the refrigerator.
They're	on	
	under	

Unit 7

Could: Requests

Could	you	pass the salt?
	I	
	he	
	she	

| How much | is…? |
| | are…? |

Unit 8

Who?

Who	is it?
	's	this?
	is	that?

| It's | Tom. | He's | a doctor. |
| | Mary. | She's | |

Color

| What color | is it? |
| | are they? |

| It's | yellow. |
| They're | |

Unit 9

Whose?

| Whose | car is it? |
| | shoes are they? |

Genitive ['s]

It	's	John's.
	is	Mary's.
		Mr. Smith's.
They	're	
	are	

Unit 10

Countable/uncountable nouns
much, many, some, any (continued)

| There | 's some | water in my glass. |
| | isn't any | |

| Is there any water in your glass? | Yes, there is. |
| | No, there isn't. |

How much water is there? There's a lot.

(Unit 10 continued)

| There | are some | apples in the refrigerator. |
| | aren't any | |

Are there any apples in the refrigerator? | Yes, there are.
| No, there aren't.

How many apples are there? There are a lot.

Unit 11

I'd like....
Would you like...?

I'd like	dessert.
I would like	a menu.
	some cheese.
	some peas.

Which?

Which	soup	would you like?
	vegetables	
	dessert	

Unit 12

Imperatives

Jump!
Go right!
Be careful!

Don't	go up the ladder.
	sit down.
	touch.
	open the door.

Object pronouns

| Put | them | on. |
| | it | |

| Take | them | off. |
| | it | |

| Turn | them | on. |
| | it | off. |

Look at	me.
	him.
	her.
	it.
	us.
	them.
	Chrissy.
	Mr. Carter.

Unit 13

What make...?/What kind...?

| What make is your car? | It's a Ford. |
| What kind of camera | is | it? | It's a Nikon. |

What kind of pens | are | they? | They're Parkers.

Unit 14

Can/Can't (ability)

I	can	drive.
You		ski.
He	can't	type.
She	cannot	dance.
It		sing.
We		swim.
They		play tennis.
		speak French.

Can	I	drive?
	you	ski?
	he	type?
	she	dance?
	it	sing?
	we	swim?
	they	play tennis?
		speak French?

Yes,	I	can.
	you	
No,	he	can't.
	she	
	it	
	we	
	they	

Unit 15

Choosing (size, color, flavor, etc.)

| Would you like | a glass of water? |
| | coffee or tea? |

Unit 16

To have + auxiliary (do/does)

I	have	a car.
You		a house.
We	don't have	a radio.
They	do not have	
He		
She	has	
It	doesn't have	
	does not have	

Do	I	have	a car?
	you		a house?
	we		a radio?
	they		
Does	he		
	she		
	it		

Yes,	I	do.
No,	you	don't.
	we	
	they	

(Unit 16 continued)

Yes,	he	does.
No,	she	doesn't.
	it	

Unit 17

To have (quantity)

What	do you	have?
How much	does she	
How many		

Unit 18

One/ones
Possessive pronouns

Which	one	's	mine?
		is	yours?
			his?
	ones	are	hers?
			ours?
			theirs?
			Anne's?

The	blue	one	's	mine.
	red		is	yours.
	small			his.
	new	ones	are	hers.
	American			ours.
				theirs.
				Anne's.

Which ones would you like?

I	'd	like	the blue ones.
You	would		
He			
She			
We			
They			

Unit 19

Requests (*May I...?, Can I...?*)

May	I	borrow	a newspaper?
Can			

Time

It's	10:00.
	4:20.

Unit 20

Describing places

What	's	New York	like?
	is		
	are	the people	

Unit 21

Present continuous (verbs without objects)

I	'm	working.
	am	sleeping.
	'm not	eating.
	am not	drinking.
He	's	sitting.
She	is	standing.
It	isn't	
	is not	
We	're	
You	are	
They	aren't	
	are not	

Am	I	working?
Is	he	sleeping?
	she	eating?
	it	drinking?
Are	we	sitting?
	you	standing?
	they	

Yes,	I	am.
	she	
	he	is.
	it	
	you	
	we	are.
	they	

No,	I	'm not.
	she	isn't.
	he	
	it	's not.
	you	aren't.
	we	
	they	're not.

Unit 22

Present continuous (verbs with objects)

What	's	she	reading?
	is	he	

She	's	reading a book.
He	is	

Who	's	she	talking to?
	is	he	
	are	you	

She	's	talking to	her	friend.
He	is		his	
I	am		my	

Who's playing football?	David is.
	David and Pamela are.

Unit 23

Requests (continued)

Can	you	show	it	to	me?
Could		give	them		him?
		bring	one		her?
			some		us?
					them?

Can	you	show	me	a camera?
Could		give	him	some pens?
		bring	her	one?
			us	some?
			them	

Unit 24

Made of

| What's | your shirt | made of? |
| What are | your jeans | |

It's	made of	leather.
They're		wool.
		silk.
		cotton.

Describing clothes/materials

It's a	short	dark	blue	nylon	skirt.
	big	light	brown	cotton	dress.
	small		gray	polyester	
	long		yellow	wool	

Too/either

He's wearing brown shoes.   She's wearing brown shoes, too.
He's a student.   She's a student, too.
He isn't a teacher.   She isn't a teacher either.

Unit 26

Time

It's a quarter to one.
It's twenty-five after one.

Unit 27

Going to future

I	'm	going to	see him	tomorrow.
	am		meet them	next week.
	'm not		eat it	next year.
	am not		drink it	
He	's		be here	
She	is			
It	isn't			
	is not			
We	're			
You	are			
They	aren't			
	are not			

(Unit 27 continued)

Am	I	going to	go there?
Is	he		be there?
	she		eat it?
	it		
Are	we		
	you		
	they		

Yes, I am.
No, I'm not.

Yes, she is.
No, she isn't.

Yes, we are.
No, they aren't.

Unit 28

Going to future (continued)

| What is she going to | do? |
| | wear? |

Unit 29

Like (present simple)

I	like	music.
You	don't like	meat.
We	do not like	dogs.
They		
He	likes	
She	doesn't like	
It	does not like	

Do	I	like	music?
	you		meat?
	we		dogs?
	they		
Does	he		
	she		
	it		

Yes, I do/No, I don't.
Yes, he does/No, he doesn't.

Unit 30

Want/need/love

I need money.
I don't need a big car.

I want a new coat.
I don't want a cup of coffee.

I love my parents.
I don't love him.

(Unit 30 continued)

Daniel loves Amy.
Who does Daniel love?
He loves Amy.

Who loves Amy?
Daniel does.

Unit 31

Asking for directions

Is there a parking lot near here?

| *Yes. Turn* | *right* | *at* | *the first traffic light.* |
| | *left* | | *the second stop sign.* |

| *Then make a* | *left.* | *It's on the* | *left.* |
| | *right.* | | *right.* |

Unit 32

Present simple (habits)

What	*do*	*you*	*do every day?*
		they	
	does	*he*	
		she	

What time	*do*	*you*	*do that?*
		they	
	does	*he*	
		she	

Unit 35

Present simple with adverbs of frequency

I	*always*	*get up*	*at seven o'clock.*
You	*usually*		
We	*often*		
They	*sometimes*		
	occasionally		
He	*hardly ever*	*gets up*	
She	*never*		

Unit 36

Present simple with adverbs of frequency (continued)

| *What time* | *do you* | *usually have dinner?* |
| *When* | *does she* | |

| *How often* | *do you* | *go out?* |
| | *does she* | |

| *What* | *do you* | *usually do after dinner?* |
| | *does she* | |

| *Do you* | *ever* | *go to the theater?* |
| *Does she* | *often* | |

Unit 37

Present simple vs. present continuous

I	*walk to work.*
	walk to work every day.
	usually walk to work.

I'm	*walking to work.*
	walking to work now.
	walking to work at the moment.

| *What* | *do you* | *do every day?* |
| | *does he* | |

| *What* | *'s he* | *doing* | *now?* |
| | *are you* | | |

Unit 38

Adverbs of manner

How	*do*	*you*	*do that?*
		we	
		they	
	does	*he*	
		she	

I	*do*	*this*	*well.*
You			*badly.*
We			*carefully.*
They			*carelessly.*
He	*does*		*slowly.*
She			*fast.*

He's a good singer/He sings well.
They're bad players/They play badly.

She's a careful driver/She drives carefully.
I'm a slow driver/I drive slowly.

Unit 39

Invitations

| *When is it?* | *On* | *Sunday* | *night.* |
| | | *etc.* | |

Present continuous for future

What	*am*	*I*	*doing*	*tomorrow?*
	are	*you*		*next week?*
		we		*next month?*
		they		*on Monday?*
	is	*he*		*on Saturday?*
		she		

I	*'m*	*going*	*out of town.*
	am		*to Washington, D.C.*
We	*'re*		*to Florida.*
You	*are*		
They			
He	*'s*		
She	*is*		

(Unit 39 continued)

Would you like to	go to	a movie?
		a baseball game?
	have	dinner?

Unit 40

Excuse	me,	how do I get to	the Canadian Falls?
Pardon		where can I find	
		I'm looking for	the Skylon Tower.

Where are | the American Falls?

| It's | behind | you. |
| | in front of | |

| They're | across | the bridge. |
| | on | your right. |

Unit 42

Past simple: *was/were*

I	was	here.
He	wasn't	there.
She	was not	
It		
You	were	
We	weren't	
They	were not	

Was	I	here?
	he	there?
	she	
	it	
Were	you	
	we	
	they	

Yes,	I	was.
	he	
	she	
	it	
Yes,	we	were.
	you	
	they	

No,	I	wasn't.
	he	
	she	
	it	
No,	we	weren't.
	you	
	they	

Unit 43

Past simple: *There was/There were*

There	was	a restaurant.
	wasn't	
	were	some hotels.
	weren't	any buses.

(Unit 43 continued)

| Was there a beach? | Yes, there was. |
| | No, there wasn't. |

| Were there any bars? | Yes, there were. |
| | No, there weren't. |

Unit 44

Past simple: *have*

I	had	breakfast.
You	did not have	a drink.
He	didn't have	dinner.
She		
We		
They		

Did	I	have	breakfast?
	you		a drink?
	he		any food?
	she		
	we		
	they		

Yes, I did.
No, I didn't.

Unit 45

Past simple: irregular verbs

I	went	to school.
You	didn't go	home.
He	did not go	
She	came	
We	didn't come	
They	did not come	

Did	I	come	to school	yesterday?
	you	go	home	last week?
	he			at 7 o'clock?
	she			on Tuesday?
	we			
	they			

Present	Past
am/is	was
are	were
have/has	had
go	went
come	came
get	got

I	got	a letter	yesterday.
You	didn't get		last Thursday.
He	did not get		this morning.
She			
We			
They			

(Unit 45 continued)

Did	I	get	a letter?
	you		
	he		
	she		
	we		
	they		

Unit 46

Past simple: regular verbs with *-ed*

I	finished	the letter.
You	didn't finish	it.
He	typed	
She	didn't type	
We	photocopied	
They	didn't photocopy	

Did	I	finish	the letter?
	you	type	it?
	he	photocopy	
	she		
	we		
	they		

Yes, I did.
No, I didn't.

Unit 48

Past simple: irregular verbs (continued)

Present	Past
see	saw
eat	ate
drink	drank
take	took

Present	Past
fly	flew
shine	shone
meet	met
write	wrote

Present	Past
ride	rode
buy	bought
bring	brought

Unit 49

Quantity: *not much, not many, a little, few*

I	have	only	a little	food.
You	had			water.
We				gas.
They			a few	crackers
He	has			books.
She	had			
It				

(Unit 49 continued)

I	don't have	much	food.
You	didn't have		water.
We			
They		many	crackers.
He	doesn't have		books.
She	didn't have		
It			

Unit 50

Past simple with adverbs of manner

I	sang	well.
You	danced	badly.
He	played	carefully.
She		quickly.
We		
They		

Unit 51

Past simple extension

I	did	that	an hour	ago.
You	saw	them	two days	
We	bought		five minutes	
They			three weeks	
He				
She				

Present	Past
find	found
give	gave
leave	left
lose	lost

Unit 52

Past simple extension

Present	Past
begin	began
burn	burned
destroy	destroyed
fall	fell
find	found
leave	left
meet	met
open	opened
send	sent
snow	snowed
speak	spoke
spend	spent

Unit 53

Past simple: question generation

Where | was | she born?

When | did | she start school?

Did | she go | into the hospital?

Past simple (continued)

Present	Past
adopt	*adopted*
become	*became*
call	*called*
die	*died*
drive	*driven*
emigrate	*emigrated*
graduate	*graduated*
hear	*heard*
investigate	*investigated*
like	*liked*
live	*lived*
major	*majored*
marry	*married*
remove	*removed*
telephone	*telephoned*
visit	*visited*

Unit 54

Present continuous vs. present simple

I'm eating in a restaurant now. I don't usually eat in restaurants.

I'm working now. I work every day.

I'm watching TV at the moment. I normally watch TV in the evenings.

Unit 55

Past continuous vs. past simple

I	was	doing the dishes.
He	wasn't	
She	was not	

Was	I	doing the dishes?
	he	
	she	

Yes,	I	was.
	he	
No,	she	wasn't.

We	were	doing the dishes.
You	weren't	
They	were not	

Were	we	doing the dishes?
	you	
	they	

(Unit 54 continued)

Yes,	we	were.
	you	
No,	they	weren't.

Unit 56

Past continuous

He | was walking to his car | when somebody hit him.

Past simple extension

Present	Past
run	*ran*
hit	*hit*
put	*put*

Unit 57

Could (past ability)
When as connector

I	could	drive	when	I	was	ten.
He	couldn't	swim		he		eighteen.
She	could not	play the piano		she		twenty.
We				we		
You				you	were	
They				they		

Could	I	swim	when	I	was	ten?
	he			he		eighteen?
	she			she		twenty?
	we			we	were	
	you			you		
	they			they		

Yes, I could.
No, I couldn't.

Unit 58

Obligation: *have to, don't have to, can't*

I	have	to	do this.
You	don't have		
We			
They			
He	has		
She	doesn't have		

Do	I	have	to	do this?
	you			
	we			
	they			
Does	he			
	she			

Yes, she does.
No, she doesn't.

Yes, you do.
No, you don't.

I	can't	do this.
You	can	
We		
They		
He		
She		

Unit 61

Present perfect

I	've	opened it.
You	have	closed it.
We	haven't	done it.
They	have not	
He	's	
She	has	
It	hasn't	
	has not	

Have	I	opened it?
	you	closed it?
	we	done it?
	they	
Has	he	
	she	
	it	

Yes, I have.
No, I haven't.

Yes, he has.
No, he hasn't.

Unit 62

Present perfect: *been, gone*

I	've	been	there.
You	have	gone	
We	haven't		
They	have not		
He	's		
She	has		
It	hasn't		
	has not		

Have	I	been there?
	you	
	we	
	they	
Has	he	
	she	

Yes,	I have.	No,	I haven't.
	he has.		he hasn't.

Where	have	I	been?
		you	gone?
		we	
		they	
	has	he	
		she	
		it	

Unit 63

Present perfect: *just, already*

I	've	just	done that.
You	have	already	painted that.
We			washed that.
They			
He/She/It	's		
	has		

do	did	done
go	went	gone
am/is/are	was/were	been
open	opened	opened
close	closed	closed
call	called	called
study	studied	studied

Unit 64

Quantity: *too much, too many, not enough*

There	's	too much	pollution.
	is		dirt.

There	are	too many	people.
	're		problems.

There	isn't	enough	fresh air.
	is not		water.

There	aren't	enough	houses.
	are not		jobs.

Unit 65

Present perfect: *yet, before*

I	've	been to Washington.
You	have	seen the Capitol.
We		
They		
He	's	
She	has	
It		

I	haven't	been to Washington	yet.
You	have not	seen the Capitol	
We			
They			
He	hasn't		
She	has not		
It			

(Unit 65 continued)

| I've | never | been to Washington | before. |
| He's | | seen the Capitol | |

| Have you | ever | been to Washington? |
| Has he | | seen the Capitol? |

| Yes, | I | have. |
| | he | has. |

| No | I | haven't. |
| | he | hasn't. |

Unit 66

Present perfect with quantity

| How | much | have you | done? |
| | many | has he | |

am/is/are	was/were	been
go	went	gone
see	saw	seen
take	took	taken
send	sent	sent
spend	spent	spent
buy	bought	bought
meet	met	met

Unit 67

Present perfect extension

Have	I	ever	done that?
	you		drunk this?
	we		seen it?
	they		eaten this?
Has	she		bought that?
	he		

| Yes, | I | have. |
| | he | has. |

| No, | I | haven't. |
| | he | hasn't. |

When	did	I	do that?
		you	drink it?
		we	see it?
		they	eat it?
		he	buy that?
		she	

drink	drank	drunk
eat	ate	eaten
drive	drove	driven
break	broke	broken
have	had	had
find	found	found
lose	lost	lost
hit	hit	hit

Unit 68

Comparatives

long	longer
short	shorter
old	older
big	bigger
wet	wetter
thin	thinner
dry	drier
heavy	heavier
large	larger
nice	nicer
good	better
bad	worse

-		+
less expensive	expensive	more expensive
less comfortable	comfortable	more comfortable
less economical	economical	more economical

Unit 69

Past obligation: *had to*

I	have to	see it.
You	don't have to	
We	had to	
They	didn't have to	
He	has to	
She	doesn't have to	
	had to	
	didn't have to	

Do	I	have to see it?
Did	you	
	we	
	they	
Does	he	
Did	she	

Yes, I do.
No, I don't.

Yes, I did.
No, I didn't.

Unit 70

Superlatives

long	longer	the longest
short	shorter	the shortest
old	older	the oldest
big	bigger	the biggest
wet	wetter	the wettest
thin	thinner	the thinnest
large	larger	the largest
nice	nicer	the nicest
dry	drier	the driest
heavy	heavier	the heaviest
good	better	the best
bad	worse	the worst

the least expensive
less expensive
expensive
more expensive
the most expensive

the least comfortable
less comfortable
comfortable
more comfortable
the most comfortable

Unit 71

Comparatives and Superlatives

The CN Tower's very tall.
It's taller than the Eiffel Tower in Paris.
It's the tallest tower in the world.

Unit 72

Offers

I'll open the window.

Requests

Will you open the window?	Of course, I will.
	No, I won't.

Suggestions

Let's go to the movies.

Why don't we go to the theater?

Unit 73

Same, different, as ... as

It's	as	cold	as	ice.
		black		night.

This car isn't	as	fast	as	that car.
		comfortable		

(Unit 73 continued)

It's	the same as	yours/ours/theirs.
They're	different from	mine/his/hers.

It's	the	most interesting	movie	I've	ever	seen.
		best/worst	play	she's		been to.
		most exciting				

Unit 74

Indefinite pronouns

	some	any?	no
Thing	something	anything?	nothing
Person	somebody	anybody?	nobody
	someone	anyone?	no one
Place	somewhere	anywhere?	nowhere

	not ... any	every
Thing	not ... anything	everything
Person	not ... anybody	everybody
	not ... anyone	everyone
Place	not ... anywhere	everywhere

Unit 75

Present perfect: *for, since*

I	've	been	here	for	two days.
You	have				a few minutes.
We					six months.
They					ten years.
He	's			since	two o'clock.
She	has				Tuesday.
It					February.

How long	have you	been	here?
	has she		there?

Unit 76

during

You can't use it	during	the flight
He was using it		the movie

apologies

I'm afraid	you can't use the computer.
I'm sorry, but	we don't have any magazines.

Unit 77

One, all, none, some, both, neither

One	of them	is happy.
Neither		
Both		are happy.
Some		
All		
None		